OVER 200 MARVELOUS RECIPES
LOW-CHOLESTEROL, LOW-FAT, LOW-SALT
AND NO SUGAR

HEALTHY

BAKING

HEAVENLY CAKES, TORTES, CHEESECAKES, PIES,
MERINGUES, CUSTARDS AND SOUFFLES

HEALTHY WHOLEGRAIN BREADS, MUFFINS,
BISCUITS, SCONES, PANCAKES,
PASTRIES, COOKIES AND SNACKS

MARVELOUS OAT BRAN MUFFINS
BREADS AND COOKIES

Florence Bienenfeld, Ph.D.
Mickey Bienenfeld

Acknowledgements

We wish to thank both Seymour R. Levin, M.D., Chief, Special Diagnostic and Treatment Unit, and Director Diabetes Clinic, Wadsworth VA Hospital, Medical Center West Los Angeles, Professor of Medicine, UCLA School of Medicine and Maylene Wong, M.D., Chief, Cardiology Noninvasive Laboratory, West Los Angeles, Veterans Administration Medical Center, Professor of Medicine, UCLA, for writing the thoughtful and informative forwards.

With great love and appreciation, we wish to thank our wonderful children, grandchildren, family and friends who encourage us with their enthusiasm for our healthy desserts and baked goods.

Published by   Royal House Publishing Co., Inc.
P.O. Box 5027
Beverly Hills, CA 90210

Printed in the United States of America
ISBN: 0-930440-33-1

The Introduction

Nothing can transform a house into a cozy home faster than the aroma of something good baking in the oven. Home baked goodies have always been synonymous with loving, gracious hospitality. Unfortunately, the ingredients used in breads, pies, cakes, and cookies have traditionally been white flour, sugar, butter, cream, sour cream, eggs, margarine and shortening, which are not considered good for you.

In white flour the healthy part of the wheat has been removed and cannot be totally replaced. White refined sugar which has been stripped of natural enzymes and nutrients, depletes and weakens the body in order to digest it. Cholesterol found in eggs, butter, cream and cheese clogs the arteries, and hydrogenated fat found in shortening and margarines is considered to be even more risky by some scientists. Salt can raise blood pressure and with it the risk of strokes.

Fortunately now it is possible to enjoy wonderful moist breads and muffins, delicious guilt-free cakes, pies, tortes and chewy cookies, and still keep healthy and fit. We have put good nutrition back into baking. HEALTHY BAKING calls for wholegrain flours, non-fat or low-fat dairy products, egg whites, little or no oil, fruit, fruit juice, yams, honey, and never salt.

You, your loved ones and friends can have the wonderful enjoyment and satisfaction of mouth-watering low-fat, low-cholesterol, low-salt, sugar-free home baked treats that are both good to eat and good for you. What a loving, nurturing way to say "I love you" to yourself and those you love and care about.

We wish you good health and good eating.

Our Warmest Regards,

Florence & Mickey Bienenfeld

Forward
Maylene Wong, M.D.

With mounting evidence that reducing blood lipids can stabilize and regress fatty deposits in arteries, and thereby put off heart attacks, it has become public policy to lower the nation's cholesterol. Preventive cardiology has become serious business and we are having to teach ourselves and our patients how to live the hygienic way of stopping cigarette smoking, controlling blood pressure, and eating cholesterol-lowering diets.

The Bienenfeld's have produced a book that should have wide appeal, not only to the high risk patient, with coronary artery disease and elevated LDL cholesterol, but to also the health-conscious who have modified their behavior and habits except for dessert. Saturated fats have long been the staple of bakery products until now. Eliminating all egg yolks and nearly all fat, and adding fiber and fruit, "Healthy Baking" reveals how to lower your cholesterol and have your cake and eat it too. And cookies, brownies, pies tortes, custards and cheesecake! For the breadmaker, there are 19 recipes for wholegrain breads and 17 for muffins, of course.

For the motivated patient, this book will be a helpful friend. For the cardiologist, the book will be a useful source and reference since the recipes are low in salt as well.

Maylene Wong, M. D.
Chief, Cardiology Noninvasive Laboratory
West Los Angeles, Veterans Administration Medical Center
Professor of Medicine, UCLA

Forward
Seymour R. Levin, M.D.

There is no question that we are attracted to the smell and taste of fats and oils in our food. We have grown to choose our menus from fat-containing items on the grocery shelf and in restaurants. If an oil has no cholesterol, we think that it is a healthy sort of fat. In fact, each gram of fat and oil gives us 9 calories, more than twice that of carbohydrates or protein.

Why, then, should the amount of fats and oils in our food concern us? Per unit of "fullness" that a meal gives us, these substances give us more calories. The greater percentage of fat in a diet which produces "fullness", the more likely may be our tendency toward obesity. Obesity, especially when coupled with conditions like diabetes or hypertension increases our risk for an earlier death than would occur if we stayed slim. Fat in our foods is, certainly, the best way to get to our hearts via our stomachs. Sixty per cent of my patients with diabetes are obese. I try to get them to convert from "steak and fries" to food that is less full of fats and oils. This should help them lose weight, bringing blood sugar, blood fat, and blood pressure more toward normal. They should be able to do this without having to take expensive courses, while receiving advice from health educators and by using books like "Healthy Baking" by the Bienenfelds. My patients need to know that they <u>can</u> have dessert but it is essential to know what <u>is or is not</u> in the dessert.

Can our patients (and those we are trying to keep from becoming patients) change their eating habits? Can they get used to enjoying the food itself without the fat in it (e.g. salad, without salad oil)? I, truly, can't answer these questions.

By preparing food plans like those in this book, Dr. Bienenfeld is not only structuring a delicious, "new" kind of food for us, she is trying to save our lives. I hope she succeeds.

Semour R. Levin, M. D.
Chief, Special Diagnostic
and Treatment Unit, and
Director Diabetes Clinic,
Wadsworth VA Hospital,
Medical Center
West Los Angeles

Professor of Medicine
UCLA School of Medicine

Important Information and Suggestions

1. Read recipe through very carefully before beginning, and assemble all ingredients called for in recipe. Preheat the oven before baking. Use level measures.

2. Use non-stick baking pans for cakes, cookies, breads and muffins. Use wooden or plastic spoons, spatulas and utensils to avoid scratching non-stick surfaces.

3. Use extra large eggs whenever egg whites are called for. Four extra-large egg whites equals 1/2 cup, 6 extra-large egg whites equals 3/4 cup, and 8 extra-large egg whites equals 1 cup. Adjustments must be made accordingly if smaller or jumbo size eggs are used. To beat egg whites, start at low speed until whites are foamy, and gradually increase speed to high. If there is any trace of yolk or fat in whites, they will not whip properly.

4. Whip low-fat cottage cheese in blender or food processor until smooth and creamy, whenever whipped cottage cheese is called for. Avoid overbaking cheesecakes made with cottage cheese or cottage cheese will curdle.

5. Use whole wheat pastry flour in cakes and breads when it is called for. In the event whole wheat pastry flour is not available in your area, whole wheat flour can be substituted, provided that the amount of flour is reduced by 2 tablespoons per cup. Baking time is increased by 5 to 10 minutes. Always test for doneness. For a moist, slightly heavy texture, use whole wheat flour.

6. It is not necessary to sift flour in any of the recipes; however, it may be necessary to put baking soda through a strainer, if it is lumpy, before adding it to dry ingredients.

7. Take care not to overbake these low-fat/cholesterol cakes and breads, or they can become too dry. Remove cakes and breads from the oven as soon as cake tester shows no sign of wet, raw, or unbaked batter. A small crumb of dry batter may still cling to tester. That's O.K. Cakes and breads become a little less moist as they cool.

8. Amount of time required for cooking or baking, and number of persons served is only approximate.

9. In recipes calling for yeast sprinkle yeast granules into warm water (105 degrees) and have all ingredients at room temperature. Refer to Instructions for Preparing Yeast Dough for more details.

10. To preserve freshness and moisture of wholegrain baked goods, especially those low in fat, store them in the refrigerator or freezer until ready for use. Before serving wrap breads, muffins, scones or pastries in foil, and reheat them in a 350-degree oven just until freshened and warm.

11. In recipes calling for wholegrain cereal flakes, use fruit-sweetened, salt-free and sugar-free products. These are available in health food stores and some markets

12. One-half non-fat milk and 1/2 non-fat yogurt can be substituted for buttermilk in recipes.

13. Use only black raisins, since golden raisins are preserved with sulfur dioxide.

14. Use only wholegrain flours and cereals. These are available in health food stores and some supermarkets.

15. Store wholegrain flours and cereals in the refrigerator until ready for use. Raw nuts can be stored in freezer.

16. Use a brand of baking powder without aluminum, available in health food stores.

17. Cold pressed oils are the most pure and wholesome, available in health food stores and some supermarkets.

18. Use frozen concentrated apple juice from sources which ban the use of alar in their products.

Instructions for Preparing Yeast Dough

1. Sprinkle yeast granules into warm water (105 degrees). A candy thermometer is advised. Hotter temperatures will kill the yeast.

2. When kneading is called for, knead the dough on a lightly floured board. Use as little flour as possible to keep dough from sticking.

3. Yeast dough should be left to rise, covered, in a warm place until double in bulk. The bowl need not be oiled.

4. To retard the yeast rising, the dough can be left to rise in the refrigerator for a number of hours or overnight.

5. For faster rising set oven at 200 degrees (not hotter) for 60 seconds only. Turn off oven, then place covered bowl with dough in oven, along with a small pot of boiling water on the same shelf. Dough will rise in 1/2 to 1/3 the usual time. This method can be repeated for both the first and second rising. The second rising may take less time than the first.

6. Dough has risen sufficiently when fingers poked 1 inch into the dough leave an indentation.

7. Dough made of whole wheat flour tends to be somewhat heavier and dryer than dough made with white flour; therefore, use as little flour as necessary, just enough to be able to handle the dough. Placing dough in the refrigerator or freezer for 30 minutes to 1 hour can make dough easier to handle or knead.

8. To avoid drying out breads and pastries follow baking instructions carefully, and do not overbake yeasted breads and pastries. They tend to become less moist as they cool.

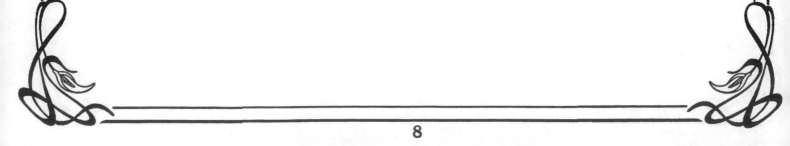

The Contents

Dedication

To the many millions
of wise health-minded men and women
who choose to be fit and still enjoy
marvelous, nutritious, low-fat, low-cholesterol
breads, muffins, cakes, custards, pies and cookies,
all packed with wholesome, natural, wholegrain goodness.

Chapter 1

Nutritious Wholegrain Breads

Bread has traditionally been called the staff of life. In days gone by it truly was. Before the 1900's breads were made from wholegrain flours which naturally supplied fiber, complex carbohydrates, vitamin B complex and vitamin E. After the 1900's the milling process began stripping away the heart or "germ" of the wheat and its fibrous outer layer we call bran, creating the bleached white flour used in most breads and pastries today.

One purpose for this change was to lighten the texture of the dough. The major purpose, however, was to prolong the shelf life of flour. Wholegrain flours cannot be stored for long periods without turning rancid. White flour can last forever, and bugs are not attracted to it either, since all of the food value has been taken out.

Our recipes put wholesome goodness back into your breads, and supply you and your loved ones, breads, muffins, pastries and delicious desserts, without added fat, cholesterol, salt and sugar.

For best results please refer to Instructions for Preparing Yeast Dough and Important Information and Suggestions found in the introduction.

Quick Whole Wheat Buttermilk Spoon Bread

This is a wholesome bread that's easy to make, and fun to eat.

1 1/2	cups whole wheat flour
2	teaspoons baking soda
1	tablespoon cinnamon

1 1/2	cups buttermilk
2	tablespoons honey
1	tablespoon lemon juice
1	teaspoon vanilla
1	teaspoon oil

4	egg whites, beaten until stiff but not dry
1/2	teaspoon oil for pan

Mix together dry ingredients, and set aside. In a large mixing bowl whisk together the next 5 ingredients until blended. Add flour mixture all at once, and mix only until smooth. Fold in beaten egg whites.

In a preheated 450-degree oven, heat a 9-inch round non-stick baking pan for 10 minutes. Remove pan from oven, oil pan lightly with 1/2 teaspoon oil, and spread batter evenly in the hot pan. Bake bread at 450-degrees for 15 to 18 minutes, or until bread tests done. Cut into wedges and serve with jam or honey. Serves 6.

Giant Round Whole Wheat Holiday Loaf
(Challah)

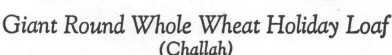

This beautiful to look at, wholesome egg bread, or challah, with raisins gives special warmth and meaning to any holiday meal. This bread can be baked ahead and frozen. On the day it is to be served, thaw it, wrap it in foil, and heat it in a 350-degree oven for 25 minutes or just until warm. Do not overbake or bread will be dry. Serve bread warm with honey.

1 1/2	cups warm water (105°)
3	envelopes active dry yeast
1/2	cup honey
6	egg whites
	grated zest of 2 small oranges
1/4	cup oil
3	cups whole wheat flour
2	teaspoons cinnamon
1 1/2	cups black raisins
1 1/2	cups whole wheat pastry flour
1/2	cup whole wheat pastry flour for kneading
1	teaspoon oil for greasing pan
1	beaten egg white for brushing on top
	sesame or poppy seeds to sprinkle on top (optional)

In a large bowl of an electric mixer stir warm water and yeast. Add next 4 ingredients and beat until blended. Beat in 3 cups whole wheat flour and cinnamon on medium speed for 5 minutes. Stop mixer, and with a wooden spoon, mix in until blended, raisins and 1 1/2 cups whole wheat pastry flour. Cover bowl and keep dough in a warm place until double in bulk.

Punch down dough, spread 1/2 cup of pastry flour on board and gently knead dough by folding it over for 1 or 2 minutes. Dough will be very soft and delicate to work with, and this will make it a finer consistency and less dry when baked. Cut dough in half. Oil bottom and sides of an 11-inch springform pan. Adding a little more flour if necessary on the board, form a thick coil. Wind this coil around in the center of baking pan. Form another coil with the remainder of the dough, and wind it around on top of the first coil, spiralling it up in the center.

Gently brush top with beaten egg white, sprinkle top with sesame seeds or poppy seeds as desired, and let dough rise in a warm place until double in bulk. Bake loaf in a 350-degree oven for 25 minutes or until top is light golden brown. Do not overbake or bread can become dry. Cool for at least 30 minutes before removing gently from pan. Yields 1 extra large size loaf.

Quick Orange Oat Bran & Wheat Bread

This tasty, wholesome bread is easy to prepare. It contains 1 1/2 cups of oat bran to keep you fit.

1 1/2	cups warm water (105°)
2	envelopes dry active yeast
3	tablespoons honey
3	tablespoons frozen concentrated orange juice, thawed
2	tablespoons oil
3	cups whole wheat flour
1 1/2	cups oat bran
1	tablespoon honey
1	tablespoon frozen concentrated orange juice

In a large mixing bowl stir yeast granules into warm water. Mix in honey, orange juice and oil, and beat with whisk until smooth. Add 1/2 of flour and mix well with whisk. Then add the last 1/2 of flour, and the oat bran. Stir with a fork until dough comes away from sides of bowl.

Do not preheat oven. Knead dough for 3 minutes on a floured board. With hands shape dough into a rectangle to fit a 9x5-inch non-stick loaf pan. Mix honey and orange juice together in a small bowl, and spread this mixture evenly on top of the dough. Place bread in a cool oven, then turn on oven to warm setting for 10 minutes. Turn oven to 400 degrees and bake bread for 20 minutes, or until bread is brown. Yields 1 loaf.

Whole Wheat Onion Flat Bread

This easy-to-prepare bread tastes great and it's so good for you.

1	tablespoon honey
1	tablespoon oil
1	tablespoon onion powder
1	cup warm water
1 3/4	cups whole wheat flour
2	teaspoons baking powder
4	tablespoons instant minced onions

In a large mixing bowl whisk together the first 4 ingredients until well blended. Mix together flour and baking powder, and stir it in with a fork until it forms a dough. Shape dough into a ball, cover with a damp towel and allow to stand at room temperature for 3 hours before baking, or for up to 8 hours in the refrigerator, if this is more convenient. Divide dough into 4 parts and form each part into a 7-inch round. Arrange flat breads on two cookie sheets, and bake in a 450-degree oven for 8 to 10 minutes. Serve warm. Yields 4 flat breads.

Whole Wheat Irish Soda Bread

This is a satisfying, wholesome bread which can be prepared in minutes.

      1 1/4   cups buttermilk
          1   tablespoon oil
        1/4   cup honey

      2 1/2   cups whole wheat flour
          2   teaspoons baking soda
          1   teaspoon cream of tartar

In a large mixing bowl whisk together buttermilk, oil and honey until blended. Mix together flour, baking soda and cream of tartar. While stirring with a fork, add the dry ingredients just until moistened. Using hands, form a dough and knead the dough in the bowl for 1 minute. If dough is too soft add a little more whole wheat flour, but as little as possible. Shape dough into a flat 7-inch circle in the middle of a non-stick cookie sheet. Cut 2 slits in top of dough 1/4-inch deep, crosswise, forming 4 quarters. Bake loaf in a 375-degree oven for approximately 35 minutes, or until deep golden brown. Yields 1 loaf.

Irish Oat and Wheat Bran Bread

This wholesome bran bread is great for toast and sandwiches.

          2   egg whites
        1/4   cup honey
      1 1/2   cups non-fat milk
          1   tablespoon oil

          2   cups whole wheat flour
      4 1/2   teaspoons baking powder
          3   tablespoons dry non-fat milk powder

      1 1/4   cups oat bran
          1   cup unprocessed Millers wheat bran

In a large mixing bowl stir together the first 4 ingredients until blended. Mix together flour, baking powder and milk powder, and add, all at once, mixing just until smooth. Do not overmix. Stir in oat bran and wheat bran, and spread batter in a 9x5-inch non-stick loaf pan. Bake bread in a 350-degree oven for approximately 65 minutes or until top is light golden brown, and bread tests done. Cool before slicing. Yields 1 loaf.

Basic Whole Wheat Bread

This wholesome wholegrain bread makes perfect sandwiches and toast.

         2   cups warm water (105°)
         2   tablespoons honey
         4   packages active dry yeast

     1 1/3   cups non-fat milk
       1/2   cup honey
         3   tablespoons oil
              grated zest of 1 large orange (orange part of the peel)

         3   cups whole wheat flour
         4   tablespoons dry non-fat milk powder
         1   tablespoon cinnamon
    4 to 5   cups whole wheat flour

In a large bowl, whisk together water, honey and yeast and set aside. In a small saucepan, heat milk until bubbles form around edges. Stir in honey, oil and grated orange zest, cool mixture until lukewarm (105°), then stir milk mixture into yeast mixture. Add next 3 ingredients, all at once, beating with a whisk for 2 minutes. Using a fork, stir in 4 cups of the whole wheat flour. Bring dough together. Use extra cup of flour as necessary to form a soft dough. (Chilling the dough for a short time will make it easier to handle.) Knead dough for 10 minutes on a lightly floured board, then return dough to bowl, cover, and set in a warm place to rise until double in bulk.

Punch dough down and cut it in half. Roll one half into a 20-inch rope. Fold the rope in thirds; flatten it down to release air bubbles, roll it up and place into a 9x5-inch non-stick loaf pan. Repeat with second half of dough. Allow dough to rise again in a warm place until doubled in bulk. Bake loaves in a 400-degree oven for 30 to 40 minutes or until tops are deep golden brown. Cool bread for at least 30 minutes before slicing. Yields 2 large loaves.

Whole Wheat Egg Raisin Twist
(Challah)

Imagine the divine aroma of this delicious, nutritious bread baking. It is the kind of bread you can enjoy on special occasions.

       3/4   cup warm water (105°)
     1 1/2   envelopes dry active yeast

       1/4   cup honey
         3   egg whites
         2   tablespoons oil

     1 3/4   cups whole wheat flour
     1 1/2   teaspoons cinnamon

       1/2   cup black raisins
              grated zest of 1 large lemon (yellow part of the peel)

(Continued)

(Whole Wheat Egg Raisin Twist, Cont.)

- 1   cup whole wheat pastry flour
- 1/2   cup whole wheat flour for kneading
- 1   egg white, beaten

In a large bowl of an electric mixer, stir yeast granules into warm water. Add next 3 ingredients, and beat on medium speed until blended. Stop mixer, add whole wheat flour and cinnamon, and beat on low speed for 5 minutes. Stir in raisins and grated zest, then fold in pastry flour until dough comes together. Cover dough and let it rise in a warm place until double in bulk.

Punch down and knead dough on floured board for 10 minutes. Cut dough into thirds and shape it into 3 thick ropes or strands, each 12 inches long. On a 10x15-inch non-stick baking sheet, braid the ropes. Brush top with beaten egg white. Let dough rise again in a warm place until double in bulk, and bake in a 350-degree oven for 20 to 25 minutes or until loaf is light golden brown. Do not overbake or bread will be dry. Yields 1 loaf.

Milk and Honey Whole Wheat Raisin Pecan Loaf

It is a pleasure to break bread with friends and loved ones, especially when the bread is beautiful to look at, and so good for you.

- 1   cup scalded non-fat milk, cooled to 105°
- 2   packages active dry yeast
- 1/3   cup honey
- 1/2   cup dry non-fat milk powder
- 4   egg whites
- 2   tablespoons oil

- 2   cups whole wheat flour
- 1   tablespoon cinnamon
- 1   cup whole wheat pastry flour

- 1   cup black raisins
- 1/2   cup chopped pecans (optional)
       grated zest of 1 small orange (orange part of the peel)

- 1   egg white, beaten

In a large bowl of an electric mixer stir yeast into the warm milk, and set aside for 10 minutes. Add next 4 ingredients to yeast mixture, and beat on high speed for 1 minute. Reduce to lowest speed and fold in 2 cups of whole wheat flour and cinnamon. Beat on medium speed for 5 minutes, then beat in whole wheat pastry flour for an additional 5 minutes. Stop mixer and fold in raisins, pecans and grated orange zest.

Place dough in a 9x5-inch non-stick loaf pan and brush top with beaten egg white. Let dough rise in a warm place until double in bulk, then bake loaf in a 350-degree oven for 25 minutes or until loaf is light golden brown. Do not overbake. Yields 1 loaf.

Onion Chile Cheese Bread

This moist, delicious and nutritious bread does not require kneading.

1/4 cup boiling water
1 teaspoon honey
2 envelopes active dry yeast

3 egg whites
1/2 cup water
1 teaspoon oil

1 cup coarsely chopped onion
1/4 cup coarsely chopped green chile peppers (or 1 4-ounce can Diced Green Chiles)
1 cup low-fat cottage cheese

2 cups whole wheat flour
2 cups whole wheat pastry flour

In a bowl mix together the boiling water and honey. Cool mixture to 105°, then stir in the yeast. Allow to stand for 20 minutes until it gets foamy. In a large bowl, whisk together next 3 ingredients until frothy, then beat in yeast mixture. Coarsely chop onion, chile peppers and cottage cheese in a food processor, and fold this into the egg white-yeast mixture. Stir in the whole wheat flour and beat well with a whisk, then add the whole wheat pastry flour, stirring with a fork until blended.

Form the dough into a ball, cover bowl with a towel, and let dough rise in a warm place until doubled in bulk. Punch down dough and place in a 9x5-inch loaf pan. Cover with towel and let dough rise again. Bake in a 350-degree oven for 45 to 55 minutes or until deep golden brown. Allow bread to cool for 15 minutes before removing bread from pan. Yields 1 loaf.

Onion Rye Bread With Caraway Seeds

1/2 cup warm water (105°)
2 packages active dry yeast

1 cup warm water
1/4 cup honey
2 tablespoons oil
2 tablespoons onion powder

2 tablespoons caraway seeds
2 cups rye flour

1 1/2 to 2 cups whole wheat flour
1/4 to 1/2 cup whole wheat flour for kneading

1 egg white for top
1 teaspoon onion powder
1 tablespoon caraway seeds for top

(Continued)

(Onion Rye Bread with Caraway Seeds, Cont.)

In the large bowl of an electric mixer stir 1/2 cup of water and yeast, and set aside for 5 minutes. Add next 4 ingredients and beat on highest speed for 1 minute. Reduce to lowest speed and add the rye flour and caraway seeds. Then add the whole wheat flour, 1/2 cup at a time. Beat dough for 5 minutes, on medium speed. Spread flour for kneading dough on a bread board, using as little flour as necessary, and knead the dough for 10 minutes.

Let dough rise, in a warm place, covered with a damp towel, until doubled in bulk. Punch dough down and form dough into 2 oval loaves (or 1 larger loaf if desired). Place loaves on a non-stick baking sheet, cover with damp towel and let dough rise again. Beat egg white and onion powder together, and brush on top of loaves. Sprinkle caraway seeds on top. Gently cut 2 slits on the top of each loaf, and bake in a 400-degree oven for 35 to 40 minutes, or until loaves are deep golden brown. Yields 2 loaves.

Whole Wheat Low-Fat Egg Bread

What a pleasure to bake breads that are wholegrain, low-fat and delicious.

- 1 1/2 cups warm water (105°)
- 3 envelopes active dry yeast

- 1/2 cup Raisin Puree (see chapter on Basics)
- 7 egg whites
- 1/2 cup frozen concentrated orange juice, thawed to room temperature
- 1/4 cup oil
  grated zest of 1 large orange (orange part of the peel)

- 3 cups whole wheat flour
- 1 teaspoon cinnamon

- 2 to 3 cups whole wheat pastry flour
- 1/2 cup whole wheat flour

- 1 beaten egg white for top
  sprinkle of sesame or poppy seeds for top

In a large bowl of an electric mixer stir yeast granules into the warm water. Add next 5 ingredients, and beat on medium speed for 1 minute. Add whole wheat flour and cinnamon, and beat on medium speed for 5 minutes. Then by hand stir in just enough of the whole wheat pastry flour to make a soft dough. Let it rise in a warm place until doubled in bulk. Punch down. Sprinkle 1/2 cup whole wheat flour on top of dough, and gently knead dough in the bowl for 1 to 2 minutes. Cut dough in half.

Place dough in two 9x5-inch non-stick loaf pans. Brush tops with beaten egg white, sprinkle with sesame or poppy seeds, and let dough rise again in a warm place until double in bulk. Bake loaves in a 350-degree oven for approximately 30 to 35 minutes, or until deep golden brown Cool for at least 20 minutes before removing loaves from pans. Yields 2 loaves.

Whole Wheat Egg Onion Twist
(Challah)

This easily prepared wholegrain bread is made with egg whites and only 2 tablespoons of oil. It has a lovely texture.

3/4	cup warm water (105°)
1 1/2	envelopes dry active yeast
1/4	cup honey
3	egg whites
2	tablespoons oil
1 1/2	tablespoons onion powder
1/8	teaspoon black pepper

1 3/4	cups whole wheat flour
1	cup whole wheat pastry flour

1/2	cup whole wheat flour for kneading
1	egg white
1	teaspoon onion powder
	sprinkle of sesame seeds for top (optional)

In a large bowl of an electric mixer stir yeast granules into warm water. Add next 5 ingredients, and beat well on medium speed until blended. Stop mixer, add the whole wheat flour, and beat on low speed for 5 minutes. Fold in pastry flour by hand. Cover dough and let it rise in a warm place until doubled in bulk. Punch dough down, and on a floured board, knead dough for 10 minutes. Then cut dough in thirds and shape it into 3 thick ropes or strands each 12 inches long.

Braid dough on a 10x15-inch non-stick baking pan. In a small bowl, with a fork, beat egg white with onion powder. Brush top with beaten egg white mixture, and sprinkle top with sesame seeds, if desired. Let dough rise again, and bake loaf in a 350-degree oven for 20 to 25 minutes, or just until it is light golden brown. Do not overbake or bread will be dry. Yields 1 loaf.

Oat Bran Black Bread

You will be amazed how satisfying this nutritious and delicious bread can be. It is packed with fiber and wholesome goodness.

2 1/2	cups water (105°)
3	envelopes active dry yeast
3	tablespoons honey
2	tablespoons dark molasses
2	tablespoons oil
4	tablespoons carob powder
1	tablespoon Postum, Cafix or other natural coffee substitute
2 1/2	cups whole wheat flour
2	cups oat bran
1	tablespoon caraway seeds
2	tablespoons raw sunflower seeds
2	tablespoons sesame seeds (optional)
1/4	teaspoon black pepper
1	cup black raisins
1/2	cup walnut chunks (optional)
	grated zest of 1 orange

1 1/2 to 1 3/4 cups whole wheat flour

In a large mixing bowl, sprinkle yeast granules into the warm water. Add next 5 ingredients, and beat well with a whisk. Stir in 2 1/2 cups of whole wheat flour and beat well, then add the oat bran, seeds, raisins, pepper, nuts and orange zest. Stir in just enough whole wheat flour until dough is not sticky. Knead dough on a lightly floured board for 10 minutes. Return dough to bowl, cover and keep in a warm place until double in bulk. Punch down and knead dough for an additional 10 minutes. Place dough in two 9x5-inch non-stick loaf pans. Cover dough and let rise again until double in bulk; then bake loaves in a 375-degree oven for approximately 35 minutes, or until tops are dark and crusty. Cool before slicing. Yields 2 loaves.

No-Knead Yam Yeast Bread

This moist delicious and nutritious bread makes great toast and sandwiches.

1 1/2	cups warm water (105°)
2	envelopes active dry yeast
1	cup whole wheat flour

8	egg whites
1/2	cup pure maple syrup
1/2	cup frozen concentrated orange juice
1	cup mashed yams (about 1 pound, baked until soft and peeled)
2	tablespoons oil

2	envelopes active dry yeast
1/4	cup warm water

2 1/2   cups whole wheat flour
2 1/2 to 3 cups whole wheat pastry flour

1	egg white
2	tablespoons fruit sweetened orange marmalade or
	2 tablespoons frozen concentrated orange juice

The night before baking this bread, in a medium-size mixing bowl, stir together the first 3 ingredients. Cover and leave this mixture in the refrigerator overnight. In the morning in a large mixing bowl whisk together the next 5 ingredients until blended. Mix together the 2 additional envelopes of yeast with water, and stir this mixture into the large mixing bowl along with the spongy yeast mixture prepared the night before. Beat well. Stir in whole wheat flour and whole wheat pastry flour with a fork, until flour is absorbed and dough comes away from the sides.

Cover bowl and let dough rise in a warm place until double in bulk. Cut dough in 2 parts, fill two 9x5-inch non-stick loaf pans. Allow dough to rise again. Mix together egg white and marmalade, and gently brush tops of loaves.

Bake loaves in a 375-degree oven for 40 to 45 minutes or until tops are dark brown. Cool in pans for 15 minutes before removing. Yields 2 loaves.

Fruit Sweetened Banana Raisin Bread

This moist easy-to-prepare bread is a delicious healthy wholegrain treat.

2 large bananas, mashed well
1/2 cup buttermilk
1 cup frozen concentrated apple juice
4 egg whites
2 teaspoons vanilla

2 1/4 cups whole wheat flour
2 teaspoons baking soda
1 teaspoon baking powder
1 tablespoon cinnamon
1/2 teaspoon coriander
1 cup black raisins

In a large mixing bowl beat the first 5 ingredients. Mix together the flour, baking soda, baking powder and spices, and add, all at once, mixing only until smooth. Do not overmix. Fold in raisins. Spread batter in a 9x5-inch non-stick loaf pan and bake in a 350-degree oven for 55 to 60 minutes, or until top is golden brown. Do not overbake. Yields 1 loaf.

Fruit Sweetened Banana Oat Bran Bread

This banana nut bread is so moist and delicious and so good for you, it's bound to become a family favorite.

1 cup mashed bananas (2 medium)
1/4 cup frozen concentrated orange juice
1/2 cup frozen concentrated pineapple juice
2 tablespoons oil
4 egg whites
1/2 cup non-fat yogurt

1 1/3 cups whole wheat flour
2 teaspoons baking soda
1 teaspoon baking powder
1/2 cup chopped walnuts (optional)
1 1/2 cups oat bran

In a large mixing bowl whisk together the first 6 ingredients until blended. Mix together flour, baking soda, baking powder and nuts, and add, all at once, mixing just until smooth. Do not overmix. Stir in oat bran.

Spread batter evenly in a 9x5-inch non-stick loaf pan. Bake bread in a 350-degree oven for approximately 45 minutes, or until top is golden brown and bread tests done. Do not overbake. Cool before slicing. Yields 1 loaf.

Moist Wholesome Corn Bread

This is a moist corn bread that is as wholesome as it is delicious.

4	egg whites
1/4	cup honey
2	tablespoons oil
1	cup non-fat milk
1	cup frozen corn kernels
1	cup whole wheat flour
1	cup cornmeal
2	tablespoons dry non-fat milk powder
4	teaspoons baking powder

In a large mixing bowl beat egg whites, honey and oil until well mixed. Blend milk and corn kernels in a blender or food processor for 1 minute. Pour corn-milk mixture into egg white mixture. Mix together flour, cornmeal, milk powder and baking powder, and add, all at once, mixing only until smooth. Do not overmix.

Pour batter into a 9x9-inch non-stick baking pan, and bake in a 425-degree oven for 18 to 20 minutes, or until top is light golden brown. Cut into squares and serve warm. Yields 9 to 12 portions.

Deluxe Banana Nut Bread

This nutritious banana bread is so good, it tastes almost like cake.

1/2	cup buttermilk or non-fat yogurt
1	tablespoon oil
1/2	cup honey
4	egg whites
2	cups pureed bananas (about 4 medium bananas)
2	teaspoons vanilla
2	cups whole wheat flour
2	teaspoons baking soda
1/2	cup chopped walnuts (optional)
1/2	cup black raisins (optional)

In a large mixing bowl whisk together the first 6 ingredients until blended. Mix together flour and baking soda and add, all at once, mixing with a whisk just until smooth. Do not overmix. Fold in nuts and raisins.

Place bread batter in a 9x5-inch non-stick loaf pan, and bake in a 350-degree oven for 55 minutes or until bread is golden brown on top and it tests done. Yields 1 loaf.

Chapter 2

Marvelous Muffins, Biscuits and Scones

Our delicious easy-to-prepare, wholegrain muffins, biscuits and scones contain only pure, wholesome ingredients. They are low in fat, cholesterol and salt; and high in fiber, vitamin B complex and vitamin E to keep you and your loved ones fit.

Most muffins, biscuits and scones are made with white flour, sugar, whole eggs, butter, margarine, shortening, sour cream, cream or whole milk. But not ours. Imagine how good it will feel to pop a batch of these marvelous muffins into the oven in just minutes, and enjoy the treat that awaits you. Knowing that they contain what your body needs to be fit will help you enjoy them even more.

Banana Oat Bran Muffins

These fruit sweetened muffins are excellent, and such a delicious way to eat your oat bran.

1 1/2	cups black raisins
2/3	cup water
2	cups pureed bananas (about 4 medium bananas)
1 1/3	cups frozen concentrated apple juice
2/3	cup non-fat or low-fat plain yogurt
8	egg whites
1	tablespoon cinnamon
1 1/2	teaspoons nutmeg
1	teaspoon coriander
1	teaspoon vanilla
2	cups whole wheat flour
2	teaspoons baking soda
1	teaspoon baking powder
2	cups oat bran

In a medium-size non-stick saucepan, cook raisins in water over low heat for 15 minutes, or until moisture is absorbed. Blend the plumped raisins in a food processor or blender. In a large mixing bowl whisk the crushed raisins, along with the next 8 ingredients, until blended. Mix together the flour, baking soda and baking powder, and add, all at once, mixing just until smooth. Do not overbeat. Stir in oat bran. Divide batter between 24 non-stick muffin cups, and bake in a 350-degree oven for 30 to 35 minutes, or until muffins test done. Serve with apple butter or fruit sweetened jam. Yields 24 muffins.

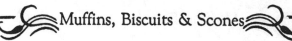

Oat Bran Carob Muffins

These moist nutritious muffins are a treat you will want to make often.

1 1/4	cups buttermilk or sour milk
1	cup frozen concentrated apple juice
2	tablespoons dark molasses
1	teaspoon vanilla
4	egg whites

1 3/4	cups whole wheat flour
1/4	cup carob powder
2	teaspoons baking soda
1 1/2	cups oat bran

In a large mixing bowl whisk together first 5 ingredients until blended and frothy. Mix together flour, carob powder and baking soda, and add all at once beating with whisk only until smooth. Do not overmix. Fold in oat bran.

Divide batter between 12 large non-stick muffin cups and bake in a 350-degree oven for 25 to 30 minutes or until muffins test done. Do not overbake. Yields 12 muffins.

Banana Blueberry Bran Muffins

These delicious, fruit sweetened muffins supply lots of bran fiber. They take only minutes to prepare, and are a healthy way to start off the day.

2	cups pureed bananas (about 4 medium bananas)
1	cup frozen concentrated apple juice
1	cup buttermilk
9	egg whites
1	tablespoon cinnamon
1	teaspoon cardamom
1	teaspoon vanilla

2	cups whole wheat flour
2	teaspoons baking soda
1	teaspoon baking powder

2	cups unprocessed Millers wheat bran
1	cup blueberries, fresh or frozen

In a large mixing bowl whisk together the first 7 ingredients until blended. Mix together flour, baking soda and baking powder, and add, all at once, mixing just until smooth. Do not overmix. Fold in bran and blueberries.

Divide batter between 24 non-stick muffin cups, and bake in a 400-degree oven for 25 to 30 minutes, or until muffins are brown. Yields 24 muffins.

Dark Moist Oat Bran Muffins

These dark, moist muffins taste almost like cake, and beside that they're so good for you.

        1 1/2   cups non-fat milk
            3   tablespoons non-fat milk powder
          1/2   cup non-fat or low-fat yogurt
          1/2   cup honey
            2   tablespoons dark molasses
            2   egg whites

            2   cups whole wheat flour plus 1 tablespoon flour
        1 1/2   teaspoons baking soda

        1 1/2   cups oat bran flakes

Whisk the first 6 ingredients in a large mixing bowl. Mix together flour and soda, and add, whisking just until smooth. Do not overmix. Stir in bran. Divide batter between 12 non-stick muffin cups and bake in a 350-degree oven for 20 to 25 minutes. Remove gently from muffin cups. Yields 12.

Deluxe Bran-Fruit Muffins

These wholesome muffins have an excellent flavor, and they are full of fruit and natural fiber to keep you feeling great. This recipe was inspired by our niece, Elaine.

            4   egg whites
          2/3   cup non-fat yogurt
            1   teaspoon vanilla
          1/3   cup frozen concentrated apple juice
            2   tablespoons dark molasses
            1   tablespoon oil

            1   cup whole wheat pastry flour
        1 1/2   teaspoons baking soda
            2   teaspoons cinnamon
        1 1/2   teaspoons nutmeg

          3/4   cup oat bran
          3/4   cup unprocessed Millers wheat bran
          1/2   cup black raisins
          1/2   cup chopped dates
          1/2   cup chopped walnuts
            1   large peach, apple, or pear, cut into bite-size pieces

In a large mixing bowl whisk together first 6 ingredients until blended. Mix together flour, baking soda and spices, and add all at once, mixing just until smooth. Do not overbeat. Fold in remaining 6 ingredients. Divide batter between 18 paper-lined muffin cups and bake muffins in a 375-degree oven for 15 minutes or until muffins test done. Yields 18 muffins.

Non-Dairy Yam Oat Bran Muffins

What a delicious low-fat way to get the fiber and wholegrain goodness your body needs!

1 1/4	cups mashed yams, baked until soft and peeled (1 1/4 pounds)
1/2	cup frozen concentrated orange juice
1/2	cup frozen concentrated pineapple juice
6	egg whites
3/4	cup hot water
1	tablespoon oil
	grated zest of 1 lemon (yellow part of the peel)

1 1/2	cups whole wheat flour
2	teaspoons baking powder
2	teaspoons baking soda
4	teaspoons cinnamon
1	teaspoon nutmeg
1/2	teaspoon ginger
2	cups oat bran

In a large mixing bowl, whisk together the first 7 ingredients until blended. Mix together flour, baking powder, baking soda, and spices, and add, all at once, mixing only until smooth. Do not overmix. Stir in oat bran.

Divide batter between 12 non-stick muffin cups and bake muffins in a 375-degree oven for approximately 30 minutes, or until muffins test done. Yields 12 muffins.

Honey Raisin Bran Cereal Muffins

These easy-to-prepare muffins are a healthy, delicious treat.

6	egg whites
3/4	cup non-fat milk
1/2	cup non-fat or low-fat yogurt
3/4	cup honey
1	tablespoon oil
1	tablespoon cinnamon

2	cups whole wheat flour
2	teaspoons baking soda
1	teaspoon baking powder

3	cups raisin-bran flakes cereal
1	cup oat bran

In a large mixing bowl whisk together first 6 ingredients until blended. Mix together flour, baking soda and baking powder, and add, all at once, mixing just until smooth. Do not overbeat. Fold in cereal flakes and oat bran. Divide batter between 12 non-stick muffin cups, and bake in a 400-degree oven for 15 to 18 minutes, or until muffins test done. Yields 12 muffins.

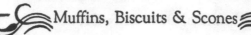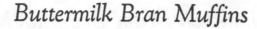
Buttermilk Bran Muffins

These are marvelous tasting bran muffins.

- 1/4 cup frozen concentrated orange juice
- 1/4 cup honey
- 3 egg whites
- 1 1/2 cups buttermilk
- 2 tablespoons oil

- 1 cup whole wheat flour
- 2 teaspoons baking powder
- 1 teaspoon baking soda
- 1/2 cup black raisins
- 2 cups raw unprocessed Millers wheat bran

In a large mixing bowl whisk together the first 5 ingredients. Mix together flour, baking powder, baking soda and raisins, and add all at once, mixing only until smooth. Fold in bran. Divide batter between 12 muffin cups, and bake in a 400-degree oven for 20 to 22 minutes. Do not overbake. Yields 12 muffins.

Blueberry Lemon Oat Bran Muffins

What a pleasure it is to prepare and serve these moist, healthful muffins for breakfast or brunch. They contain 2 cups of oat bran. Just what the doctor ordered.

- 1/2 cup frozen concentrated orange juice
- 1/2 cup frozen concentrated pineapple juice
- 6 egg whites
- 2/3 cup buttermilk
- 1 tablespoon oil
- grated rind or zest of 1 lemon
- 1 teaspoon lemon juice

- 1 1/4 cups whole wheat pastry flour
- 2 teaspoons baking powder
- 2 teaspoons baking soda
- 2 teaspoons cinnamon
- 1/2 teaspoon coriander
- 2 cups oat bran
- 1 1/2 cups frozen blueberries, unthawed

In a large mixing bowl whisk together the first 7 ingredients until smooth. Mix together flour, baking powder, baking soda and spices, and add all at once, mixing only until smooth. Stir in oat bran, then frozen blueberries. Divide batter between 12 non-stick muffin cups, and bake in a 375-degree oven for 25 to 28 minutes. Yields 12 muffins.

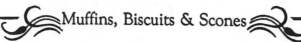

Yam-Pineapple Oat Bran Muffins

These non-dairy fruit and yam sweetened muffins are the yummiest ever.

1 1/2	cups mashed yams, baked until soft and peeled (1 1/2 pounds)
6	egg whites
1/3	cup frozen concentrated orange juice
2/3	cup frozen concentrated pineapple juice
1	cup water
1	tablespoon oil
2	teaspoons cinnamon
1/2	teaspoon nutmeg
1/2	teaspoon ginger
1/8	teaspoon cloves
1	cup whole wheat flour
2	teaspoons baking powder
1	teaspoon baking soda
2	cups oat bran
1/2	cup black raisins
1/4	cup chopped walnuts (optional)

In a large mixing bowl whisk together first 10 ingredients until well blended. Mix together flour, baking powder, and baking soda and add all at once, whisking just until smooth. Stir in oat bran, raisins and nuts. Do not overmix. Divide batter between 12 non-stick muffin cups and bake in a 375-degree oven for about 40 minutes, or until light golden brown. When cool store in refrigerator or freezer. Yields 12 muffins.

Orange, Banana, Pineapple Oat Bran Muffins

1	cup banana slices (2 medium-large bananas), packed down solidly
1/2	cup frozen concentrated orange juice
1/2	cup frozen concentrated pineapple juice
6	egg whites
3/4	cup buttermilk
1	tablespoon oil
	grated zest of 1 large orange (orange part of the peel)
1 1/4	cups whole wheat flour
2	teaspoons baking powder
2	teaspoons baking soda
1/4	cup dry non-fat milk powder
1	tablespoon cinnamon
1/2	teaspoon coriander
1/2	cup black raisins
2	cups oat bran

Whisk together first 7 ingredients until blended. Whisk in remaining ingredients until blended. Divide batter between 18 non-stick muffin cups, and bake at 375° for 18 to 20 minutes. Yields 18 large muffins.

Wheat-Free Banana Honey Oat Bran Muffins

These wholesome muffins have a great texture and flavor, and they contain oats and oat bran instead of wheat flour.

1 2/3	cups pureed bananas (about 3 large bananas)
1/2	cup honey or Raisin Puree (see chapter on Basics)
	grated zest of 1 lemon (yellow part of the peel)
	grated zest of 1 orange (orange part of the peel)
6	egg whites
3/4	cup buttermilk
1	tablespoon oil
2 1/2	cups rolled oats
2	teaspoons baking powder
2	teaspoons baking soda
1/4	cup dry non-fat milk powder
1	tablespoon cinnamon
1/2	teaspoon coriander
1/2	cup black raisins
2	cups oat bran
1/2	cup chopped walnuts (optional)

In a large mixing bowl whisk together the first 7 ingredients until blended. Grind oats until very fine in a blender or food processor. **Measure out 1 1/4 cups of the ground oats.** Mix together the 1 1/4 cups of ground oats with baking powder, baking soda, milk powder, spices and raisins. Stir dry ingredients into bowl, mixing only until blended. Do not overmix. Stir in oat bran just until moistened.

Divide batter between 18 non-stick muffin cups and sprinkle nuts on top. Bake in a 400-degree oven for 15 minutes or until muffins test done. Do not overbake. Let muffins cool for 10 minutes before removing. Yields 18 large muffins.

Orange Popovers

6	egg whites
3/4	cup non-fat milk
1/4	cup frozen concentrated orange juice
1	tablespoon oil
1	cup whole wheat flour

Heat a 12-cup non-stick muffin pan in a 450-degree oven for 10 minutes. Meanwhile in a large mixing bowl whisk together first 4 ingredients until blended and frothy. Add flour and stir only until smooth. Do not overmix. Divide batter between 12 muffin cups, and bake in a 450-degree oven for 20 minutes. **Reduce oven temperature to 325-degrees and continue baking** popovers for 5 minutes longer. Turn off oven and let popovers remain in oven for 30 minutes before removing. Serve warm with your favorite fruit sweetened jam. Yields 12.

 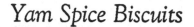
Yam Spice Biscuits

These delicious, wholesome biscuits are delicately spiced. Serve them pipping hot with honey or your favorite fruit sweetened jam.

1	cup mashed yams, baked until soft and peeled. (You will need 1 pound.)
1	tablespoon oil
4	egg whites
1	teaspoon cinnamon
1/2	teaspoon ginger
1/4	teaspoon cloves
1	teaspoon lemon juice
2	cups whole wheat flour
1 1/2	teaspoons baking soda
1	tablespoon natural cream of tartar

Blend the first 7 ingredients in a food processor or blender until smooth. Turn this mixture into a large mixing bowl. Mix together the flour, baking soda, and cream of tartar, and add all at once, mixing just until smooth. Bring the soft dough together in the bowl.

On a floured board press the dough out into a circle 3/4-inch thick with hands. Cut biscuits with a biscuit cutter or glass, and place on a non-stick cookie sheet. Bake in a 450-degree oven for 12 minutes or until light brown on top. Yields 12.

Quick Hot Biscuits

You can enjoy these low-fat mouth-watering wholegrain biscuits in just minutes.

1/2	cup low-fat cottage cheese
4	egg whites
1/3	cup non-fat milk
2	tablespoons honey
1	tablespoon oil
1	teaspoon grated lemon or orange zest
2 1/2	cups whole wheat flour
1	tablespoon baking powder

In a large mixing bowl whisk together first 6 ingredients until blended. Mix together flour and baking powder, add flour gradually, while stirring with a fork, until flour is blended. With dough still in bowl, bring dough together with hands, then roll out 1/2 of dough at a time on a floured board into a circle 1/2 inch thick. Cut rounds with a glass or biscuit cutter, and arrange biscuits on a non-stick baking sheet. Bake biscuits in a 450-degree oven for 8 to 10 minutes. Enjoy with your favorite fruit sweetened jam. Yields 12 to 16.

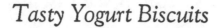

Tasty Yogurt Biscuits

These flavorful, nutritious biscuits take just minutes to prepare.

    1   cup non-fat or low-fat yogurt
    2   tablespoons oil
    2   tablespoons honey
         grated zest of 1 lemon (yellow part of the peel)

    2   cups whole wheat flour
    1   tablespoon baking powder
   1/2   teaspoon baking soda

In a large mixing bowl whisk together the first 4 ingredients until well mixed. Mix together flour, baking powder and baking soda, and add gradually while stirring with a fork until flour is blended. Using hands, bring dough together and knead it for 1 minute. On a board flatten dough into a circle 1-inch thick. Cut into 8 biscuits with a biscuit cutter or glass. Bake in a 450-degree oven for 12 to 15 minutes or until deep golden brown. Yields 8 biscuits.

Easy Large Orange Scones With Currants

These delicious wholesome scones taste every bit as great as rich buttery scones do, and without the cholesterol and salt.

  1 1/4   cups buttermilk (or non-fat or low-fat yogurt)
   1/3   cup frozen concentrated orange juice
    3   egg whites
    2   tablespoons oil

  3 1/2   cups whole wheat flour
    2   tablespoons natural cream of tartar
    1   tablespoon baking soda
    1   cup black currants (or black raisins)

In a large mixing bowl whisk together the buttermilk, orange juice, egg whites and oil until blended. Mix together flour, cream of tartar and baking soda, and add 1/2 of the dry ingredients to the buttermilk mixture, mixing only until smooth. Stir in raisins, then the remainder of the dry ingredients just until blended. Do not overmix. Drop batter onto non-stick baking sheets into mounds, 1 inch high by 3 inches in diameter. Arrange scones 1/2 inch apart, and bake them in a 450-degree oven for 15 minutes or until golden brown on top. Yields 15 large scones.

Chapter 3

Fabulous Guilt-Free Cakes and Tortes

Imagine being able to indulge and enjoy heavenly cakes and tortes without having to feel guilty afterwards. Now you can, because our delicious wholegrain cakes and tortes are good food and good for you.

The cakes and tortes in this section are rich-tasting, delicious and guilt-free. Ingredients called for are all pure wholesome foods, such as wholegrain flour, egg whites, fruits, fruit juices, honey, vegetables, non-fat or low-fat dairy products, carob powder, and spices. Fat, cholesterol, sugar, and salt are left out, and the wonderful natural flavors, aroma and appeal are left in.

Here you have a wide variety of cakes and tortes to choose from. It will make you feel so good to be able to take good care of your body and your sweet tooth, all at the same time.

Holiday Currant Cake

This beautiful, healthy cake is a special treat around the holidays, and so easy to prepare.

3/4	cup honey
1 2/3	cups orange juice (or 1/3 cup frozen concentrated orange juice and 1 1/3 cups water)
2	cups currants or black raisins
4	egg whites
1	tablespoon lemon juice
	grated zest of 1/2 lemon (yellow part of the peel)
	grated zest of 1/2 orange (orange part of the peel)
2 1/2	cups whole wheat flour
2	teaspoons baking soda
1	teaspoon baking powder
1	tablespoon cinnamon
2	teaspoons nutmeg
1/2	teaspoon coriander
1/2	cup walnuts (optional)

In a 4 to 5-quart saucepan bring honey, juice and raisins to a boil. Lower heat and cook, uncovered, for 10 minutes. In a large mixing bowl combine next 4 ingredients. Beat with whisk until frothy, then stir in honey-raisin mixture. Mix together flour, baking soda, baking powder, and spices, and mix in, 1/2 at a time, stirring only until blended. Fold in nuts, and spread batter evenly in a 10-inch tube pan. Bake in 350-degree oven for 40 minutes or until cake tests done. Serves 10 to 12.

Light Apple Torte

This delicious, innocent fruit sweetened torte is a healthy version of the rich tortes of Europe. You can enjoy this one without guilt.

Torte Shell:
1	cup whole wheat flour
1 1/2	teaspoons baking powder

4	egg whites
1	cup frozen concentrated apple juice
2	teaspoons cinnamon
1/4	teaspoon coriander

Glazed Apple Slices:
4	medium size red or golden delicious apples
1	tablespoon lemon juice

1/2	cup frozen concentrated apple juice
1	teaspoon cinnamon
1/2	teaspoon coriander

Sift flour and baking powder together and set aside. In the large bowl of an electric mixer, beat together next 4 ingredients on highest speed for 1 minute and on medium speed for 1 minute. Reduce speed to lowest setting and gently fold in flour and baking powder. Pour batter into a 10-inch springform pan, and bake in a 350-degree oven for 25 minutes. It will fall as it bakes and form a torte shell.

Wash and peel apples. Cut each apple into 16 slices. In a large bowl toss apple slices with lemon juice and set aside. In a 4 to 5-quart covered saucepan, mix together next 3 ingredients. This size pan is necessary to avoid juice boiling over. Add apple slices and cook over medium heat, covered, stirring occasionally for 7 minutes, then remove cover and continue cooking for 5 minutes longer, stirring occasionally, until apple slices are fork tender and juice is thick and syrupy. Stir gently so that slices do not break.

Cool apple slices and torte shell, then decorate top of torte with apple slices as follows: Overlapping apple slices, make a circle 1/2 inch from the outer edge of the shell. Next overlap apple slices to make an inner circle, and finally overlap apple slices in center. The inner circle will look like petals of a flower. Drizzle remaining syrup from apple slices evenly over the top. Store in refrigerator and serve cold or at room temperature. Serves 6 to 8.

Lemon Pudding Cake with Lemon Honey Sauce

For an unusual treat, try this delicious lemony pudding cake that bakes with its own sauce. To save time prepare Lemon-Honey Sauce first.

Lemon-Honey Sauce:
1	cup boiling water
1/3	cup lemon juice
1	cup honey
2	tablespoons cornstarch or potato starch
2	tablespoons cold water

To prepare sauce: In a 4 to 5-quart non-stick saucepan, bring the first 3 ingredients to a boil. Reduce heat to medium and continue cooking the sauce for 7 to 10 minutes. (Be careful as the sauce could boil over.) Mix together cornstarch or potato starch and cold water, and stir into mixture, stirring constantly, until sauce thickens. Remove sauce from heat and set aside.

Lemon Pudding Cake Batter:
1	cup mashed yams, baked until soft and peeled (1 pound)
1/4	cup lemon juice
1/3	cup frozen concentrated pineapple juice
1/3	cup frozen concentrated orange juice
	grated zest of 1 large lemon (yellow part of the peel)
2	tablespoons oil
6	egg whites
2	cups whole wheat pastry flour
2	teaspoons baking powder
2	teaspoons baking soda
2	tablespoons dry non-fat milk product

To prepare cake batter: In a large mixing bowl whisk together first 7 ingredients. Mix together flour, baking powder, baking soda and milk solids, and add, all at once, mixing only until smooth. Spread batter in a 9x13-inch glass oven-proof baking dish, and smooth top.

Spoon sauce on top of the cake batter, covering the cake batter completely. Bake cake in a 325-degree oven for 30 to 35 minutes, or until sauce on top is thick, but still moist. Do not overbake. Serve warm or cold. Serves 12 to 16.

Carob Fudge Pudding Cake

Its hard to imagine how a cake can be so fudgy and rich-tasting and still be so innocent and wholesome. You have to taste it to believe it.

1	cup pitted dates, packed down
1	cup black raisins, packed down
1	cup boiling water
1	teaspoon dark molasses
1	teaspoon vanilla
4	egg whites
2	tablespoons oil
1	cup non-fat milk
2	cups whole wheat pastry flour
4	teaspoons baking soda
1/4	cup carob powder
2	tablespoons dry non-fat milk powder
3/4	cup walnut chunks (optional)

Carob Honey Sauce:

1 3/4	cups boiling water
2/3	cup carob powder
1	cup honey
1	teaspoon molasses
1	teaspoon vanilla

In a medium-size non-stick saucepan, cook dates and raisins in boiling water over medium heat until mixture boils. Reduce heat to low and simmer for 5 minutes. Remove from stove, and cool for 5 minutes. Puree date-raisin mixture in a food processor or blender, and place this mixture in a large mixing bowl. Whisk in next 5 ingredients until blended. Stir together next 5 ingredients and add it to the bowl, stirring until blended. Do not overmix. Spread cake batter evenly into a 9x13-inch glass oven-proof baking pan.

To Make Carob Honey Sauce: In a medium-size non-stick saucepan dissolve carob powder in boiling water. Stir in honey, molasses and vanilla. Bring sauce to a boil, reduce heat and boil for 5 minutes. Be careful the sauce does not boil over. Spoon sauce on top of the cake batter, covering the cake batter completely.

Bake cake in a 325-degree oven for 25 to 35 minutes, or just until sauce on top is thick, but still moist. Do not overbake. Cake can be served warm or cool. Store in refrigerator or freezer if desired. Serves 12 to 16.

Banana Orange Layer Cake With Creamy Orange Frosting

This is a delightfully light, flavorful treat. If desired, arrange banana slices, tossed in lemon juice, between cake layers and on top of cake.

- 1 cup sliced bananas, packed down solidly
- 1/3 cup frozen concentrated orange juice
- 1/3 cup frozen concentrated pineapple juice

- 1/4 cup buttermilk or non-fat yogurt
- 2 tablespoons oil
- 2 teaspoons cinnamon
- 1/2 teaspoon coriander
- 2 tablespoons honey

- 2 cups whole wheat pastry flour
- 2 teaspoons baking powder
- 2 teaspoons baking soda
- 1/2 cup walnut chunks (optional)

- 8 egg whites

Blend bananas, orange juice and pineapple juice in a blender or food processor until smooth. Place mixture in a large mixing bowl, and whisk in the next 5 ingredients until blended.

Mix together flour, baking powder, baking soda and walnuts, and stir in, all at once, just until smooth. Whip egg whites until stiff but not dry, then fold in whites 1/3 at a time. Spread cake batter evenly in two non-stick 9x1/2-inch round cake pans. Bake in a 325-degree oven for 30 minutes, or until layers begin to separate from sides of pan. Cool layers before frosting cake. Yields two 9-inch layers.

Creamy Orange Frosting:
- 1/4 cup frozen concentrated orange juice
- 1/4 cup honey
- 1/3 cup boiling water

- 2 cups low-fat cottage cheese
- 1 tablespoon cornstarch or potato starch
- 1 tablespoon cold water

In a medium-size non-stick saucepan bring honey, orange juice and boiling water to a boil, reduce heat and cook for 7-10 minutes. Whip cottage cheese in a blender or food processor, and let whipped cheese remain in blender. Mix together starch and cold water, and add this mixture to bubbling mixture in saucepan, stirring constantly until thick and shiny. Cool for 5 minutes, then add honey and orange mixture to whipped cottage cheese in blender, and whip until smooth. Frost center first, then top and sides. Yields enough frosting for one 9-inch layer cake.

Lemon Layer Cake With Creamy Low-Fat Lemon Frosting

This cake is a special treat that is deliciously innocent.

- 3/4 cup mashed yams, baked until soft and peeled (3/4 pound)
- 1/3 cup frozen concentrated orange juice
- 1/3 cup frozen concentrated pineapple juice

- grated zest of 1 lemon (yellow part of the peel)
- 1/4 cup lemon juice
- 2 tablespoons oil
- 2 tablespoons honey

- 2 cups whole wheat pastry flour
- 2 teaspoons baking powder
- 2 teaspoons baking soda
- 2 tablespoons dry non-fat milk powder
- 8 egg whites

Puree yams, orange juice and pineapple juice in a blender or food processor. Place mixture in a large mixing bowl, along with the next 4 ingredients.

Mix together flour, baking powder, baking soda and milk powder, and fold dry ingredients into yam mixture, mixing as little as possible. Batter will be quite thick. Beat egg whites until stiff, but not dry. Gently fold beaten whites into cake batter 1/3 at a time. Spread batter evenly into two non-stick 9x1/2-inch round cake pans. Bake layers in a 325-degree oven for 25 to 30 minutes, or until cake layers begin to separate from the sides of the pan. Cool before frosting cake. Yields two 9-inch layers.

Creamy Low-Fat Lemon Frosting:
- 1/3 cup boiling water
- 2 tablespoons lemon juice
- 1/3 cup honey

- 1 tablespoon cornstarch or potato starch
- 1 tablespoon cold water
- 2 cups low-fat cottage cheese

In a medium size non-stick saucepan bring the first 3 ingredients to a boil, lower heat and cook for 7 to 10 minutes. Mix together cornstarch and water, and add to bubbling mixture in saucepan, while stirring constantly until mixture is thick and clear. Remove from stove and cool for 5 minutes. Whip the cottage cheese in a blender or food processor. Add lemon-honey mixture to whipped cottage cheese and whip until smooth and creamy. Yields enough frosting to frost center, top and sides of one 9-inch layer cake.

Carrot-Spice Layer Cake
with Creamy Honey Spice Frosting

This wholesome delicious cake is likely to become a favorite of yours, as it is ours.

1 1/2	cups cooked, soft mashed carrots (about 3/4 pound)
1/2	cup frozen concentrated orange juice
1/2	cup frozen concentrated pineapple juice
2	tablespoons oil
2	teaspoons vanilla
1	tablespoon honey

2	cups whole wheat pastry flour
2	teaspoons baking soda
2	teaspoons baking powder
1	tablespoon cinnamon
1	tablespoon nutmeg

1/2	cup black raisins
1/2	cup walnut chunks (optional)
8	egg whites, beaten until stiff but not dry

Blend first 6 ingredients in a blender or food processor. Place this mixture in a large mixing bowl. Mix together flour, baking soda, baking powder and spices, and add all at once stirring only until dry ingredients are absorbed. Stir in raisins and nuts, then gently fold in stiffly beaten egg whites 1/3 at a time. Spread cake batter evenly in two non-stick 9x1/2-inch round cake pans. Bake in a 325-degree oven for 30 to 35 minutes, or until layers begin to separate from sides of pan. Cool layers before frosting cake. Yields two 9-inch layers.

Creamy Honey Spice Frosting:

1/3	cup boiling water
1/2	cup honey
1	teaspoon cinnamon
1	teaspoon nutmeg

1	tablespoon cornstarch or potato starch
1	tablespoon cold water
1	teaspoon vanilla
2	cups low-fat cottage cheese

In a medium size non-stick saucepan bring the first 4 ingredients to a boil. Reduce heat and cook mixture for 7 to 10 minutes. Mix together starch, cold water, and vanilla, and add to bubbling mixture in saucepan, stirring constantly until mixture is thick and shiny. Remove from stove and cool for 5 minutes. Whip cottage cheese in a blender or food processor. Beat in lemon honey mixture until smooth. Yields frosting for one 9-inch layer cake.

Carob Custard Party Torte

This torte is a delicious, delicate, low-fat, low-cholesterol dessert treat.

Carob Torte Shell:

5	tablespoons carob powder
5	tablespoons whole wheat pastry flour
1/2	cup honey
2	teaspoons dark molasses
2	teaspoons vanilla
10	egg whites
1	tablespoon carob powder for bottom of pan
1/2	cup unsalted, shelled pistachio nuts, chilled for garnish (optional)

Sift carob powder and flour after measuring and set aside. In a small mixing bowl stir honey, molasses and vanilla, and set aside. In a large bowl of an electric mixer beat egg whites on high speed until foamy. Gradually add the honey, molasses and vanilla, beating until whites are stiff enough to stand in soft peaks but not dry. Reduce speed to lowest setting and gently fold in carob powder-flour mixture with a spatula just until blended.

Sprinkle the bottom of an 11-inch spring form baking pan with 1 tablespoon of carob powder. Gently spread the carob meringue mixture along the sides of pan and the remainder evenly on the bottom, forming a torte shell. Bake torte shell in a 375-degree oven for 20 minutes or until shell is light brown. Allow torte shell to cool in pan, then cover it and place it into the refrigerator or freezer as desired. Fill torte shell with Carob Cream Custard and return to refrigerator or freezer. If frozen let torte thaw for 20 minutes before serving. Serve partially thawed. Garnish with chilled pistachio nuts. Serves 10 to 12.

Carob Cream Custard:

3	cups non-fat milk
4	tablespoons dry non-fat milk powder
3/4	cup carob powder
1/2	cup plus 2 tablespoons whole wheat pastry flour
6	egg whites
1/2	cup honey
1	tablespoon dark molasses
1	tablespoon Postum powder, Cafix or other natural coffee substitute
1	tablespoon cornstarch or potato starch
1	tablespoon vanilla, or rum (optional)

In a large bowl of an electric mixer beat the first 9 ingredients on high speed until well blended. Pour carob mixture into the top of a double boiler. Over rapidly boiling water stir custard frequently with a wire whisk until custard becomes very thick. Remove from heat, cool for 5 to 10 minutes, then blend custard in a food processor or blender until velvety smooth. Add vanilla or rum, and chill in refrigerator before filling torte shell.

Best Banana Raisin Cake

This moist fruit sweetened banana cake is both delicious and nutritious. You can feel good about serving it to your friends and loved ones.

2	cups pureed ripe bananas (about 4 medium bananas)
1/2	cup frozen concentrated orange juice
1	tablespoon oil
4	egg whites
1	tablespoon cinnamon
1/2	teaspoon coriander
1	cup buttermilk
2	teaspoons vanilla

3	cups whole wheat pastry flour
2	teaspoons baking soda
1	teaspoon baking powder
1	cup black raisins

4	egg whites

In a large bowl of an electric mixer, beat first 8 ingredients for 2 minutes on medium speed. Mix together flour, baking soda and baking powder. On lowest speed fold in dry ingredients, 1/2 at a time, just until blended. Do not overmix. Fold in raisins. In a small bowl of an electric mixer whip remaining 4 egg whites until stiff but not dry. Fold these in gently.

Spread cake batter evenly in a 10-inch spring form baking pan, and bake in a 375-degree oven for 60 minutes or until cake is brown and tests done. Serves 12 to 16.

Two-Layer Carob Date Pecan Fudge Party Cake

You will feel so proud to serve this luscious rich-tasting, health cake at your next party or for your family at any time.

1	teaspoon oil
1	recipe Fruit-Sweetened Carob Brownies (see index)
1	recipe Date Carob Fudge Frosting (see chapter on Basics)

Spread 1/2 teaspoon oil into each of the two 9 x 1-1/2-inch round non-stick cake pans and set aside. Prepare the Fruit Sweetened Carob Brownie batter, substituting chopped pecans for the walnuts. Reserve 1/4 cup of the chopped pecans to sprinkle on top of the frosted cake. Spread the batter evenly into the prepared cake pans, and bake layers in a 400-degree oven for 12 to 15 minutes. Do not overbake or the layers may become dry. Cool layers in pan.

Meanwhile, prepare frosting as directed, adding an extra tablespoon of boiling water to make spreading easier. Carefully loosen sides and bottoms of both layers. Gently place 1 layer onto cake plate. Spread with 1/2 the frosting. Top with 2nd layer and spread with remaing frosting. Sprinkle top with reserved pecans. Refrigerate cake until serving time. Serves 12 to 16.

Guilt-Free Holiday Pumpkin Spice Fruit Cake

This easy-to-prepare, deliciously moist, fruit cake is made with whole wheat flour and contains no fat, cholesterol, salt or sugar. It makes perfect healthy, inexpensive gifts for the holiday season.

2	cups canned pumpkin puree
1	cup honey
4	egg whites
1	tablespoon cinnamon
1	teaspoon nutmeg
1	teaspoon ginger
1	teaspoon coriander
1/4	teaspoon cloves

2 3/4	cups whole wheat flour
2	teaspoons baking soda
1	teaspoon baking powder

1	(20-ounce) can crushed pineapple, drained
1	(15-ounce) box black raisins
1	cup chopped walnuts (optional)

In a large mixing bowl whisk together pumpkin, honey, egg whites and spices. Mix together flour, baking soda and baking powder, and add to pumpkin mixture, mixing just until blended. Stir in pineapple, raisins and nuts. Spread batter evenly in a 10-inch tube pan and bake in a 325-degree oven for 1 hour and 15 to 30 minutes or until tester comes out clean. Allow cake to cool in pan before removing it. Serves 12 to 16.

Ginger Spice Cake

This nutritious cake has a delicious spicy flavor.

1/2	cup dark molasses
1	tablespoon oil
1/4	cup honey
1	cup non-fat yogurt or buttermilk
1/2	cup frozen concentrated orange juice
7	egg whites

2 3/4	cups whole wheat pastry flour
2	teaspoons baking soda
1	tablespoon ginger
1/2	teaspoon cinnamon
1/2	teaspoon nutmeg
1/2	teaspoon cloves

In a large mixing bowl, whisk together first 6 ingredients until blended. Mix together flour, baking soda and spices and add, 1/2 at a time, mixing only until smooth. Do not overmix. Pour cake batter into a 10-inch springform pan, and bake in a 350-degree oven for 45 minutes or until cake tests done. Allow cake to cool before serving. Serves 12.

Old World Applesauce Cake

The marvelous flavor and aroma of this cake will awaken your taste buds, and keep them happy through every mouthful.

    1 1/2   cups Homemade Cinnamon Applesauce (see chapter on Basics)
        2   tablespoons oil
        1   cup frozen concentrated apple juice
        1   tablespoon cinnamon
            grated zest of 1 lemon (yellow part of the peel)

        2   cups whole wheat pastry flour
        2   teaspoons baking powder
        1   teaspoon baking soda

      1/2   cup black raisins
      1/2   cup chopped walnuts (optional)
        6   egg whites, beaten until stiff but not dry

In a large mixing bowl, whisk together the first 5 ingredients. Mix together flour, baking powder and baking soda, and add all at once, mixing with a whisk only until smooth. Stir in raisins and nuts, then gently fold in beaten egg whites. Do not overmix. Spread batter in a 10-inch spring form baking pan. Bake in a 350-degree oven for 1 hour and 5 to 10 minutes, or until center of cake tests done. Store in refrigerator or freezer. Serves 12.

Poppy Seed Spice Cake

If you're fond of poppy seeds, you're sure to enjoy this light, flavorful fruit-sweetened cake.

      3/4   cup frozen concentrated orange juice
      3/4   cup frozen concentrated pineapple juice
      1/2   cup water
        2   tablespoons oil
        2   teaspoons vanilla

        2   cups whole wheat pastry flour
        2   teaspoons baking soda
        2   teaspoons baking powder
        1   tablespoon cinnamon
        1   teaspoon nutmeg
      2/3   cup poppy seeds
        8   egg whites, stiffly beaten, but not dry

In a large mixing bowl, whisk together first 5 ingredients until blended. Mix together flour, baking soda, baking powder, spices and poppy seeds, and add, all at once, mixing just until smooth. Gently fold in stiffly beaten egg whites and spread batter evenly in a 10-inch tube cake pan. Bake cake in a 350-degree oven for 55 to 60 minutes. Invert cake pan immediately until cake is cool. Serves 10.

Yam Spice Cake

This marvelous, moist cake is flavored deliciously with yams, bananas and fruit juice, and delicately spiced. If served warm, this cake is like a delicious spicy pudding cake. It can be served as such. As the cake cools it then becomes less moist and can be sliced.

- 8 egg whites

- 2 cups mashed yams, baked until soft and peeled (2 pounds)
- 2 cups pureed bananas (about 4 medium bananas)
- 1/2 cup frozen concentrated orange juice
- 1/2 cup frozen concentrated pineapple juice
- 1 tablespoon oil

- 3 1/2 cups whole wheat pastry flour
- 2 teaspoons baking soda
- 1 teaspoon baking powder
- 1 teaspoon nutmeg
- 1/2 teaspoon cloves
- 1 teaspoon ginger
- 1 tablespoon cinnamon

In a large mixing bowl beat whites with a whisk until frothy. Puree yams in a food processor or blender, and add to the egg whites. Stir in pureed bananas, orange and pineapple juices and oil, and beat with a whisk until blended.

Mix together next 7 ingredients, and fold into egg white mixture, 1/2 at a time, stirring gently only until smooth. Do not overmix. Spread batter into a 10-inch tube pan, and bake in a 350-degree oven for 1 hour and 15 minutes. Do not overbake. Serves 12 to 16.

Three-Layer Date Carob Fudge Cake

You and your guests will be amazed that such a luscious, rich-tasting fudge cake can be made without fat, cholesterol or sugar. You can truly enjoy this cake to your heart's content.

- 1 recipe Fruit Sweetened Carob Brownies (see Index)
- 1 recipe Date Carob Fudge Frosting (see chapter on Basics)
- 1/2 cup chopped pecans or walnuts, (optional), toasted in a 350-degree oven for 8 minutes

Prepare Fruit Sweetened Carob Brownie batter as directed, omitting the walnuts. Bake this brownie layer for only 12 minutes. Do not overbake. Remove from oven and cool layer while preparing the Date Carob Fudge Frosting.

Prepare frosting recipe as directed, then spread frosting over the entire brownie layer while it is still in the baking pan. Cut this layer into 3 equal size rectangular layers, each 5x10-inches. Loosen bottom of brownie layer gently with a spatula before removing. Stack layers, one on top of the other, on a cake plate or serving platter. Sprinkle top with chopped nuts (optional). Refrigerate until ready to serve. Cut cake into slices with a sharp knife. Serves 12 to 16.

Deluxe Almond & Raisin Torte

For a special splurge this elegant, rich-tasting crunchy almond torte is just marvelous.

- 1 1/2 cups raw almonds, soaked in cold water for several hours or overnight in refrigerator

- 3 egg whites
- 1/4 cup honey
- 1 1/2 cups raisins
  grated zest of 1 lemon (yellow part of the peel)
- 2 teaspoons vanilla
- 1 tablespoon oil

- 3/4 cup whole wheat pastry flour
- 1 teaspoon baking soda
- 2 teaspoons cinnamon

- 6 egg whites
- 1 teaspoon lemon juice

- 1 teaspoon oil for pan

Drain soaked almonds, then grind them in a blender or food processor as finely as possible in batches if necessary. Reserve 1/4 cup of ground almonds for top of torte. Place remaining ground almonds in a large mixing bowl. In a blender or food processor, blend the next 6 ingredients for 3 minutes, then add this mixture to ground almonds in the mixing bowl. Mix together pastry flour, baking soda and cinnamon, and add, all at once, stirring just until dry ingredients are moistened.

In a large bowl of an electric mixer beat egg whites and lemon juice until stiff but not dry. Gently fold whites into batter 1/3 at a time, spread torte batter into a lightly oiled 10-inch springform pan, and sprinkle reserved almonds on top. Bake in a 350-degree oven for 30 to 35 minutes, or just until cake tests done. Do not overbake. This cake should be moist. Serves 10.

Carob Carrot Spice Cake

The carrots, spices and fruit juices in this moist carob cake gives it an exciting flavor and aroma.

- 6 egg whites
- 1/2 cup frozen concentrated orange juice
- 1/2 cup frozen concentrated pineapple juice
- 3/4 teaspoon dark molasses
- 1 cup non-fat milk
- 1/2 cup non-fat or low-fat yogurt
- 1 tablespoon oil
- 2 teaspoons vanilla

(Continued)

(Carob Carrot Spice Cake, Cont.)

```
2    cups whole wheat pastry flour
1    tablespoon baking soda
3/4  cup carob powder
4    teaspoons cinnamon
2    teaspoons ginger
1/2  teaspoon cloves

3    cups grated carrots
1/2  cup raisins
1/2  cup chopped nuts (optional)
```

In a large mixing bowl, whisk together the first 8 ingredients. Mix together flour, soda, carob powder and spices, all at once, whisking just until blended. Do not overbeat. Stir in carrots, raisins and nuts.

Bake cake in a 350-degree oven for 1 hour and 10 to 15 minutes in a 10-inch round spring form baking pan. The cake is done when a cake tester comes out clean. Do not overbake. Serves 12.

Carob Cupcakes

These light delicious cupcakes are great to keep on hand in the freezer for lunches and snacks. Date Carob Fudge Frosting is a lovely, optional topping.

```
1 3/4  cups boiling water
1      cup carob powder

9      egg whites
1      cup honey
1/4    cup dark molasses
1      teaspoon cinnamon
1/2    cup non-fat milk powder
1      cup non-fat milk
1/2    cup non-fat or low-fat yogurt
1      tablespoon vanilla
1      tablespoon oil
2      tablespoons Postum, Cafix or other natural coffee substitute

3      cups whole wheat pastry flour
1      tablespoon baking soda
1      teaspoon baking powder
```

In a large mixing bowl, whisk together hot water and carob powder until smooth. Add next 10 ingredients and whisk until blended. Mix together flour, baking soda and baking powder, and stir in dry ingredients just until smooth. Do not overbeat.

Divide batter between 30 paper-lined muffin cups and bake in a 350-degree oven for 18 to 20 minutes. Do not overbake. Yields 30 cupcakes.

Best Low-Fat Carrot Cake

Imagine a moist carrot cake, full of whole-grain goodness and with only 1 tablespoon of oil. If desired, use Creamy Honey Spice Frosting (see Index.)

2   egg whites
1/2   cup honey
1   cup frozen concentrated apple juice, thawed
1   tablespoon oil
2   teaspoons vanilla

2   cups whole wheat flour
2   teaspoons baking soda
1   teaspoon baking powder
1   tablespoon cinnamon
1   tablespoon nutmeg

3   cups grated carrots, solidly packed
1/2   cup chopped walnuts (optional)
3/4   cup black raisins
6   egg whites, beaten to soft peaks
1   teaspoon oil for pan

Whisk first 5 ingredients in a mixing bowl. Whisk in next 5 ingredients until blended. Do not overmix. Stir in carrots, walnuts and raisins just until blended. Fold in beaten egg whites just until blended. Lightly oil a 9x13-inch non-stick baking pan and spread batter evenly. Bake at 350-degrees for 40 minutes or until cake tests done. Do not overbake. Serves 16.

Light Hazelnut Torte

This elegant dessert is sweetened entirely with dates and raisins.

1 1/2   cups pitted dates, packed down solidly
1/2   cup black raisins
3   egg whites
2   teaspoons vanilla
1   tablespoon oil

1   cup whole wheat pastry flour
1   teaspoon baking soda
2   teaspoons cinnamon
1/2   cup chopped hazelnuts (or pecans)

6   egg whites
1   teaspoon cider vinegar
1   teaspoon oil for pan
1/4   cup chopped hazelnuts for top

In a food processor, finely grate first 5 ingredients and place in a large bowl. Mix together next 4 ingredients and set aside. Beat egg whites with vinegar until stiff. Fold 1/3 of the whites into the date-raisin mixture, then fold in the remainder of the whites. Fold in the dry ingredients just until blended.

Gently spread batter in a 10-inch lightly oiled springform pan, and sprinkle chopped hazelnuts on top. Bake in a 350-degree oven for 30 minutes, or until light golden brown on top. Serves 8 to 10.

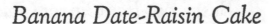

Banana Date-Raisin Cake

3	cups pureed bananas (about 6 medium bananas)
1	cup pitted dates, packed down solidly
1 1/3	cups black raisins
2	tablespoons oil
4	egg whites
	grated zest of 1 large lemon (yellow part of the peel)
2	teaspoons lemon juice

1 1/2	cups whole wheat pastry flour
1/4	cup cornstarch or potato starch
2	teaspoons baking soda

8	egg whites
1/2	teaspoon cream of tartar
1/2	cup chopped pecans
1	teaspoon oil for pan

Place bananas in a bowl. Finely chop next 6 ingredients in a food processor and stir into bananas. Fold in next 3 ingredients just until blended. Beat egg whites with cream of tartar until stiff. Fold whites into batter 1/3 at a time, then fold in nuts. Spread batter into an oiled 10-inch springform pan. Bake at 350° for 50 to 60 minutes, or until top is brown and cake tests done. When warm, this cake is like a souffle. It will fall as it cools. Serves 12.

Cherry Carob Party Cake

This is a moist delicious fudge-like cake that is a great dessert.

1	16-ounce package frozen dark pitted cherries, partially thawed
1	cup frozen concentrated apple juice, partially thawed
3	tablespoons honey
1	tablespoon oil
6	egg whites
1	teaspoon dark molasses
1	teaspoon almond extract
1	teaspoon vanilla

3/4	cup carob powder
2	cups whole wheat pastry flour
2	teaspoons baking powder
1	teaspoon baking soda
2	tablespoons dry non-fat milk powder
1/2	cup boiling water
1/3	cup sliced almonds (optional)

Reserve 1 cup whole cherries, and in a food processor, coarsely chop remainder. Whisk together next 7 ingredients until blended. Stir in whole and crushed cherries. Whisk in remaining ingredients until blended. Place batter in a 10-inch springform pan and bake at 350° for 60 minutes, or until cake tests done. Do not overbake. This cake should be moist. Serves 10 to 12.

Chapter 4

Luscious Low-Cholesterol Cheesecakes, Meringues, Custards and Souffles

Most cheesecakes are made with cream cheese, sour cream, whole eggs, butter and sugar. They are very high in both cholesterol and fat, just what your body does not need. Imagine being able to prepare and serve beautiful, divine-tasting low-cholesterol, low-fat cheesecakes, made innocently with low-fat cottage cheese, egg whites, fruit juices or honey, and natural flavorings.

Imagine being able to prepare luscious souffles and mouth-watering meringues filled with creamy non-fat puddings or fruit fillings. There is even a recipe here for an elegant trifle containing no fat or cholesterol at all.

Our easy-to-prepare cheesecakes and souffles are delicious and you won't feel stuffed after eating them. This is because they are made with good food that is low in fat. It is not unusual for us to eat a big piece of nutritious cheesecake in place of our usual breakfast or lunch, especially when we are on the run. Our cheesecakes also make nutritious snacks for children. The first words our young grandson, Adam, says when he walks into our house are, "Did you make me a cheesecake, Grandma?"

Orange Custard Bread Pudding

This healthy and delightful bread pudding can be served warm or cold for a breakfast or brunch, or as a dessert. The grain in the bread, with the milk and egg whites, provide a nourishing protein dessert.

8	slices of soft whole wheat bread, crusts removed
1	cup non-fat milk
4	tablespoons dry non-fat milk powder
6	egg whites
1/3	cup frozen concentrated orange juice
1/3	cup honey
1	tablespoon whole wheat flour
1	teaspoon vanilla
1	teaspoon cinnamon
1 2/3	cups non-fat milk
1/4	cup black raisins
	sprinkle of nutmeg

Cut bread slices into 1/2-inch cubes and set aside. Blend next 8 ingredients in a blender or food processor until smooth. Pour mixture into a large mixing bowl, and stir in remaining milk, raisins and bread crumbs. Pour the custard mixture into a 9x9-inch glass oven-proof baking pan. Sprinkle with nutmeg. Bake bread pudding in a 375-degree oven for 30 to 35 minutes or until custard is set and begins to puff up slightly. Serves 6.

Carob Pecan Souffle With Low-Fat Honey Vanilla Sauce

It is hard to believe that these wholesome ingredients can be transformed into such a delicious gourmet taste treat.

1/2	cup carob powder
1/4	cup dry non-fat milk powder
1	tablespoon instant coffee substitute (such as Postum or Cafix)
1/2	cup boiling water
1 1/2	teaspoons dark molasses
2	cups non-fat milk
1	tablespoon oil
1/2	cup honey
1/4	teaspoon cinnamon
1/4	cup corn starch or potato starch
1/4	cup whole wheat pastry flour
1	teaspoon vanilla, or 1 teaspoon rum extract (optional)
1/2	cup chopped pecans (optional)
8	egg whites, beaten until stiff but not dry
2	tablespoons chopped pecans for top

In a large bowl, dissolve carob, milk, and coffee substitute in boiling water. Add next 5 ingredients and beat with a whisk until blended. Whisk in flour and cornstarch just until smooth. Cook mixture in top of double boiler over rapidly boiling water, stirring occasionally. Once it begins to thicken then stir constantly until thick like a pudding. Remove from stove, and stir in vanilla or rum extract, and return it to mixing bowl. Stir in chopped pecans, then gently fold in beaten egg whites.

Gently spread souffle mixture in a 2-quart souffle dish, sprinkle pecans on top and bake souffle in a 375-degree oven for 25 to 30 minutes or just until souffle is puffed, set, and light brown. Serve immediately with Low-Fat Honey Vanilla Sauce over each portion. Serves 4 to 6.

Low-Fat Honey Vanilla Sauce:

4	egg whites
1/4	cup honey
1	teaspoon vanilla extract
1/3	cup non-fat milk
1	tablespoon dry non-fat milk powder

Whisk all the ingredients in the top of a double boiler over gently simmering water until thickened. Sauce will thicken quickly once the water below is boiling. Do not allow sauce to boil. When sauce has thickened, puree it in blender or food processor until smooth. Refrigerate until serving.

Strawberry Dream Souffle

This fluffy innocent souffle has its own delicious strawberry sauce on the bottom. The sauce can be made ahead of time if desired. This souffle takes only 15 minutes to bake, and what a dessert treat it is!

Strawberry Sauce:
- 1   20-ounce package frozen strawberries
- 1/2   cup frozen concentrated apple juice
- 2   tablespoons honey
- 1/4   teaspoon coriander
- 1 1/2   tablespoons cornstarch or potato starch

In a medium-size non-stick saucepan, slowly heat the sauce ingredients, until mixture comes to a boil. Allow sauce to simmer for 5 minutes, stirring occasionally. Cool sauce and puree it in a blender or food processor until smooth. Reserve 1 cup of sauce, and spread the remainder on the bottom of a 2-quart souffle dish.

Strawberry Meringue:
- 8   egg whites, at room temperature, no trace of egg yolk
- 1/4   cup honey
- 1   tablespoon cornstarch or potato starch
- 1   cup Strawberry Sauce

Twenty minutes before serving, preheat oven to 375-degrees. Beat egg whites in the large bowl of an electric mixer until foamy. Gradually beat in honey until whites are stiff but not dry. Reduce speed to low and gently fold in starch and reserved sauce. Gently spread egg white mixture into souffle dish over Strawberry Sauce. Bake in a 375-degree oven for 15 minutes or until souffle is puffed and light brown on top. Serve immediately. Cut large slices of meringue and spoon sauce from bottom of souffle dish over each serving. Serves 4 to 6.

Luscious Low-Cholesterol Cheesecake with Strawberry Glaze

Cheesecake and berries go together. You will feel so good knowing this cheesecake is minus cream cheese, egg yolks, and sugar.

4	cups low-fat cottage cheese
3/4	cup honey
1 1/2	teaspoons vanilla
1/4	teaspoon almond extract
1	tablespoon lemon juice
	grated zest of 1/2 medium lemon (yellow part of the peel)
2	tablespoons whole wheat pastry flour
2	tablespoons cornstarch or potato starch
6	egg whites

In a food processor or blender, whip cottage cheese, in batches if necessary, until smooth. Place whipped cottage cheese in a large mixing bowl. Blend remaining 8 ingredients in a food processor or blender for 30 seconds, and stir this mixture into whipped cottage cheese until well blended. Pour into prepared Crushed Cereal Flakes Crust. Bake cheesecake in a 325-degree oven for 30 to 35 minutes, or until cheesecake is puffed slightly around edges. Do not overbake. Cheesecake will set as it cools. Chill until serving. Serves 8.

Crushed Cereal Flakes Crust:

1	cup wheat flakes or corn flakes
2 1/2	tablespoons frozen concentrated apple juice
1	teaspoon cinnamon
1/2	teaspoon coriander

In a blender or food processor coarsely chop the cereal flakes with remaining crust ingredients. Pat mixture evenly on the bottom of a 9x9-inch glass oven-proof baking pan. Bake in a 325-degree oven for 10 to 12 minutes or just until set, but not browned.

Strawberry Glaze and Whole Fresh Strawberries:

1 1/2	cups frozen whole strawberries, unsweetened
3	tablespoons cornstarch or potato starch
1/3	cup frozen concentrated apple juice
2	boxes of large strawberries

Heat first 3 glaze ingredients in a small non-stick saucepan, and cook until glaze is thick and shiny. Gently spread glaze over cheesecake. Wash strawberries, cut off stems and dry berries well. Stand whole strawberries, cut side down in the strawberry glaze, beginning at corners and outer edges first and arranging berries evenly on top of cheesecake.

The Ultimate Low-Cholesterol After-Theater Cheesecake

This cheesecake is a very special treat. It tastes like the kind made with cream cheese and eggs, but instead it is made with low-fat cottage cheese and egg whites. So enjoy.

Whole Wheat Lemon-Honey Crust:
 1   cup whole wheat flour
 1   teaspoon grated lemon zest

 1   teaspoon lemon juice
 1   egg white
 2   teaspoons water
 2   tablespoons honey
 2   tablespoons oil
1/2   teaspoon vanilla

 1   tablespoon frozen concentrated orange juice, thawed

In a medium size mixing bowl mix together flour and grated zest. In a small bowl mix together next 6 ingredients, and add this mixture gradually to the flour, stirring with a fork until liquid is blended. Form dough into a ball and press dough down in the bottom of a 10-inch springform pan. Working from the inside outward, press the dough toward the edges covering the seam, so that it is well sealed. Brush the concentrated orange juice evenly on top of crust to act as a glaze. Bake crust in a 400-degree oven for 10 minutes.

Cheesecake Batter:
 5   cups low-fat cottage cheese at room temperature

 1   cup honey
1/4   cup whole wheat pastry flour
1/4   cup cornstarch or potato starch
1/4   cup dry non-fat milk powder
     grated rind or zest of 1 medium lemon
     grated rind or zest of 1 medium orange
1/2   teaspoon vanilla
 11   egg whites

Preheat oven to 500-degrees. In a blender or food processor whip cottage cheese until very smooth. Place whipped cheese in a large mixing bowl. Next blend all remaining ingredients, in batches if necessary, and pour mixture into the whipped cottage cheese. Whisk together well until thoroughly mixed.

Pour cheesecake batter into prepared crust, and bake for 10 minutes in a 500-degree oven. Reduce heat to 250-degrees and bake for 60 minutes longer. Cool cheesecake, then chill it for at least 3 hours before serving. Serves 10 to 12.

Low-Cholesterol Party Apple Cheesecake

The combination of apples and cheese has traditionally been an elegant touch to end a meal. This scrumptious, healthy, low-cal and low-cholesterol dessert is bound to bring raves from family and friends.

> 2 cups finely chopped wheat flake or corn flake crumbs
> 2 tablespoons concentrated apple juice
> 1 teaspoon cinnamon
> 1/2 teaspoon coriander
>
> 8 cups sliced delicious apples (may be sliced in food processor)
> 1/2 cup concentrated apple juice
> 2 teaspoons cinnamon
> 1 teaspoon coriander
> 1/2 cup chopped pecans (optional)
>
> 5 1/2 cups low-fat cottage cheese, whipped
> 1/2 cup low-fat plain yogurt
> 1 1/4 cups honey
> 1/3 cup potato starch or cornstarch
> 2 teaspoons lemon juice
> 1/2 teaspoon almond extract
> 1 teaspoon vanilla
> 9 egg whites
>
> sprinkle of nutmeg and coriander

Mix together first 4 ingredients and spread on bottom of a 9x13-inch baking pan. In a large mixing bowl, toss the apple slices in apple juice with cinnamon, coriander, and pecans. Spread the apple slices evenly on top of cereal mixture in baking dish. Cover with foil, and poke 8 to 10 small holes in the foil with a sharp knife. Bake in a 425-degree oven for 30 minutes, or until apple slices are softened. Discard foil.

While apple slices are baking combine next 8 ingredients in a large mixing bowl and mix well with whisk until smooth. After apple slices are softened remove baking dish from oven, pour cheesecake batter over apple slices, and sprinkle top with nutmeg and coriander. **Reduce oven temperature to 325-degrees** and bake cheesecake for 30 minutes longer, or just until cheesecake is set. Do not overbake. Filling will thicken as it cools. Remove apple cheesecake from oven. Cool and refrigerate. Serves 12 to 16.

Fluffy Low-Fat Pineapple Cheesecake
With Honey Pineapple Sauce

Pineapple and cottage cheese seem to go together. This delicious, light cheesecake is one of our favorites.

        1   cup crushed unsweetened pineapple

        4   cups low-fat cottage cheese

    1/2   cup honey
    1/3   cup frozen concentrated pineapple juice, unsweetened
    1/4   teaspoon coriander
        3   tablespoons cornstarch or potato starch
        3   tablespoons whole wheat pastry flour

        6   egg whites, beaten until stiff but not dry

Drain crushed pineapple well. Reserve juice for Honey Pineapple Sauce. Meanwhile prepare cheesecake batter: Whip cottage cheese until smooth and creamy in a food processor or blender, in batches if necessary. Place the whipped cottage cheese in a large mixing bowl. Blend next 5 ingredients in the food processor or blender, and add this mixture to the whipped cottage cheese. Beat with a whisk until well mixed. Stir in crushed pineapple, then gently fold in stiffly beaten egg whites 1/3 at a time. Pour cheesecake mixture into the prepared Pineapple Granola Crust, and bake in a 325-degree oven for 1 hour. Then turn off oven and leave cheesecake in the oven with door closed for 1 hour longer. Cool before refrigerating. Serves 8 to 10.

Pineapple Granola Crust:
        1   cup Fruit Sweetened Oat Bran Granola (see chapter on Basics),
                or commercial brand of granola
        2   tablespoons frozen concentrated pineapple juice
        1   tablespoon water

In a blender or food processor crush granola with juice and water. Press mixture in a 10-inch springform baking pan, covering edge well, and extending crust mixture 1/2 inch up the sides. Spread remaining mixture sparingly on the bottom. Bake crust in a 325-degree oven for 15 minutes, or until crust is set.

Honey Pineapple Sauce:
        1   cup unsweetened pineapple juice, reserved from drained crushed
                pineapple
        2   tablespoons honey
        1   tablespoon water
        1   tablespoon cornstarch or potato starch

Heat all sauce ingredients in a small non-stick saucepan, stirring constantly until sauce thickens. Chill and serve over slices of Fluffy Low-Fat Pineapple Cheesecake.

Blueberry Party Cheesecake

This beautiful, creamy delicious low-fat cheesecake is a pleasure to serve and a delight to eat.

Cheesecake Filling:

6	cups low-fat cottage cheese
1	cup honey
2	teaspoons vanilla
1/4	teaspoon almond extract
1	tablespoon lemon juice
	grated zest of 1/2 lemon (yellow part of the peel)
4	tablespoons cornstarch or potato starch
4	tablespoons whole wheat pastry flour
1 1/4	cups egg whites

In a blender or food processor, whip cottage cheese, in batches, until very smooth and place in a large mixing bowl. Blend remaining filling ingredients in food processor or blender until smooth, and stir this mixture into the whipped cottage cheese. Pour cheesecake batter into prepared Cereal Flake Nut Crust. Bake in a 325-degree oven for 55 to 60 minutes or until cheese filling is set, slightly puffed at edges and light brown. Remove from oven and cool. Meanwhile prepare Blueberry Glaze.

Cereal Flake Nut Crust:

2	cups wheat flakes or corn flakes
1/2	cup walnut chunks (optional)
3	tablespoons concentrated apple juice, thawed
1	teaspoon cinnamon
1/2	teaspoon coriander

In a food processor or blender, coarsely chop walnuts with wheat flakes. In a medium size mixing bowl mix together cereal-nut mixture, apple juice and spices. Spread crust mixture evenly on the bottom and 1/2-inch up the sides of a 10-inch spring form baking pan. Bake crust in a 325-degree oven for 10 minutes. Cool crust for 10 minutes, then gently shake out any loose crumbs.

Blueberry Glaze:

4	cups frozen blueberries, unsweetened
2	tablespoons cornstarch or potato starch
1/2	cup frozen concentrated apple juice
1/4	cup water
1/4	teaspoon coriander

In a 4 to 5-quart saucepan, heat all glaze ingredients, stirring constantly, until mixture thickens and becomes clear. This will happen rather quickly. Stir slowly so the blueberries will remain whole. Cool glaze for 10 to 15 minutes, then gently spread glaze on top, working from outer edges inward. Serves 10 to 12.

Elegant Low-Cholesterol Cheesecake

This cheesecake is easy to prepare. It tastes so rich and delicious, your guests would never be able to guess it is made with low-fat cottage cheese.

Whole Wheat Pineapple Walnut Crust:
- 1   cup whole wheat flour
- 1   teaspoon grated orange zest (orange part of the peel)
- 1/4   cup chopped walnuts

- 1   egg white
- 1   tablespoon honey
- 1   tablespoon frozen concentrated pineapple juice
- 1   tablespoon water
- 2   tablespoons oil
- 1/2   teaspoon vanilla

- 1   tablespoon frozen concentrated pineapple juice

In a medium-size mixing bowl mix together flour, zest and chopped walnuts. In a small bowl mix together next 6 ingredients, and stir this mixture gradually into the flour until blended. Press dough on the bottom and 1/2-inch up the sides of a 10-inch springform pan, carefully sealing the seam. Brush the concentrated pineapple juice evenly on top of the crust to act as a glaze. Bake crust in a 400-degree oven for 10 minutes. Meanwhile prepare cheesecake filling.

Cheesecake Batter:
- 6   cups low-fat cottage cheese

- 9   egg whites
- 3   tablespoons cornstarch or potato starch
- 3   tablespoons whole wheat pastry flour
- 1   tablespoon lemon juice
     grated rind of 1 lemon
- 1   cup honey
- 1 1/2   teaspoons vanilla
- 6   drops almond extract

Preheat oven to 400-degrees. In blender or food processor, whip cottage cheese in batches until very smooth. Place whipped cottage cheese into a large mixing bowl. In food processor, blend remaining ingredients for 30 seconds and stir into whipped cottage cheese.

Pour batter into a prepared Whole Wheat Pineapple Walnut Crust. Bake cheesecake in a 400-degree oven for 25 minutes. Turn off oven and let cheesecake remain in oven for 2 to 3 hours. Refrigerate until time to serve. Serves 10 to 12.

The Ultimate Carob Mocha Cheesecake

You'll find no cholesterol or coffee in this rich-tasting, delicious carob mocha cheesecake. This special dessert has become a favorite of ours.

Carob Walnut Crust:

1	teaspoon dark molasses
2	tablespoons honey
1/2	teaspoon vanilla
1	egg white
2	tablespoons water
1	tablespoon oil
1	cup whole wheat flour
1	tablespoon carob powder
1/4	cup chopped walnuts (optional)

In a medium-size mixing bowl, whisk together the first 6 ingredients until well blended. With a fork, stir in flour, carob powder and walnuts until flour is blended. Form dough into a ball, then place it into the center of a 10-inch springform pan. Working from the center, pat the dough on the bottom and 1/2-inch up the sides of the pan, carefully sealing the seam. Bake crust in a 400-degree oven for 15 minutes.

Mocha Cheesecake Filling:

5	cups low-fat cottage cheese
1	cup honey
1/4	cup dry non-fat milk powder
3	tablespoons carob powder
3	tablespoons whole wheat pastry flour
1/3	cup cornstarch or potato starch
2	teaspoons natural coffee substitute (Postum, Cafix or other)
1	teaspoon dark molasses
2	teaspoons vanilla
11	egg whites

Preheat oven to 500-degrees. In a blender or food processor blend cottage cheese until smooth and creamy. Place whipped cottage cheese into a large mixing bowl. Blend remaining ingredients in blender or food processor, in batches, until smooth. Whisk honey-egg white mixture into cottage cheese until blended.

Pour cheese filling into prepared Carob Walnut Crust and bake cheesecake for 10 minutes in 500-degree oven. Reduce oven temperature to 250 degrees, and bake cheesecake for 1 hour longer. Remove from oven, cool, and refrigerate cheesecake for 3 hours or overnight. Before serving remove sides of springform pan and cut slices with a sharp knife. Serves 10 to 12.

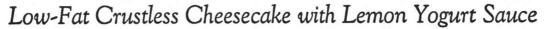

Low-Fat Crustless Cheesecake with Lemon Yogurt Sauce

At last, here is a divine tasting cheesecake you can feel good about eating. The preparation takes only minutes.

4   cups low-fat cottage cheese

1/2   cup honey
1   teaspoon vanilla
1/4   teaspoon almond extract
1   tablespoon lemon juice
grated zest of 1/2 lemon (yellow part of the peel)
1   tablespoon whole wheat pastry flour
2   tablespoons cornstarch or potato starch
6   egg whites

In a food processor or blender, whip cottage cheese, in batches if necessary, until smooth. Place whipped cheese in a large mixing bowl. Blend the next 8 ingredients for 30 seconds, and stir this into the cheese mixture. Pour batter into a 9x9-inch glass oven-proof baking pan, and bake cheesecake in a 325-degree oven for 25 to 35 minutes, or just until cheesecake begins to puff around edges. Remove cheesecake from the oven, cool for 15 to 20 minutes and then refrigerate until serving. Serve with Lemon Yogurt Sauce spooned on top. Serves 8 to 10.

Lemon Yogurt Sauce:
1 1/2   cups plain yogurt, non-fat or low-fat
3   tablespoons fresh lemon juice
2   tablespoons honey

Mix ingredients together and chill. Yields 1 3/4 cups of sauce.

Fluffy Low-Fat Orange Cheesecake

This excellent cheesecake is sure to bring raves.

4   cups low-fat cottage cheese
1/3   cup frozen concentrated orange juice
1/2   cup honey
3   tablespoons cornstarch or potato starch
2   tablespoons whole wheat pastry flour

6   egg whites, beaten until stiff but not dry

In a food processor or blender, in batches if necessary, whip cottage cheese until smooth and creamy . Place the whipped cottage cheese in a large mixing bowl. Blend next 4 ingredients in the food processor or blender, and add this mixture to the whipped cottage cheese. Beat with a whisk until well mixed. Gently fold in stiffly beaten egg whites 1/3 at a time. Pour cheesecake mixture into the prepared Orange Granola Crust, and bake in a

(Continued)

(Fluffy Low-Fat Orange Cheesecake, Cont.)

325-degree oven for 50 minutes. Then turn off oven and leave cheesecake in the oven with door closed for 1 hour before removing it from oven. Cool before refrigerating. Serves 8 to 10.

Orange Granola Crust:
- 1 cup Fruit Sweetened Oat Bran Granola (see chapter on Basics), or commercial brand of granola
- 2 teaspoons frozen concentrated orange juice
- 1 tablespoon water

In a blender or food processor coarsely chop granola with juice and water. Press mixture into a 10-inch springform pan, sealing the seam and extending the crust mixture 1/2-inch up the sides. Spread remaining mixture sparingly on the bottom. Bake crust in a 325-degree oven for 15 minutes, or until crust is set.

Low-Fat Cherry Cheesecake (Crustless)

This delicious cheesecake is satisfying and easy to prepare.

- 4 cups low-fat cottage cheese (2 pounds)

- 2 tablespoons cornstarch or potato starch
  grated zest of 1/2 lemon (yellow part of the peel)
- 1 tablespoon lemon juice
- 1/4 teaspoon almond extract
- 1 teaspoon vanilla
- 6 egg whites
- 1/4 cup frozen concentrated apple juice
- 1/4 cup honey

Whip cottage cheese in a food processor or blender until smooth. Place whipped cottage cheese in a large mixing bowl. Blend remaining ingredients in food processor or blender in batches if necessary. With a whisk stir this mixture into the whipped cottage cheese in mixing bowl until thoroughly blended. Pour cheesecake mixture into a 9x9-inch glass oven-proof baking pan, and bake cheesecake in a 325-degree oven for 25 minutes, or until sides are slightly puffy. Do not overbake. Cheese filling will set as it cools. Refrigerate and serve chilled with Cherry Topping. Serves 8.

Cherry Topping:
- 1 12-ounce package frozen pitted dark sweet cherries
- 1/3 cup frozen concentrated apple juice
- 1/4 teaspoon coriander
- 1 tablespoon cornstarch or potato starch

Heat all ingredients in a non-stick saucepan, stirring constantly until mixture thickens. Cool, for a few minutes, then starting at outer edges, gently spread topping evenly on top of cheesecake and chill.

Giant Carob Mocha Party Meringue

This rich-tasting elegant dessert contains no cholesterol.

1   Giant Soft Meringue Party Shell (see chapter on Basics)
    double recipe Carob Mocha Pudding (see Index)
1   cup chopped pecans or pistachio nuts, toasted

Prepare and bake meringue shell according to instructions, and chill meringue on baking sheet in refrigerator. The meringue can be made the day before serving.

Prepare a double recipe of Carob Mocha Pudding. As soon as the pudding is at room temperature, gently spread the pudding evenly over the meringue, leaving a 1-inch border. Sprinkle nuts evenly on top, and chill until serving. Serves 12.

Giant Strawberry Cream Party Meringue

For a light, elegant, mouth-watering dessert without cholesterol, this is it. This meringue is filled with Flavorful Vanilla Pudding, topped with fruit-sweetened berry preserves and fresh sliced strawberries or sliced almonds.

1   Giant Soft Meringue Party Shell (see chapter on Basics)
    double recipe of Flavorful Vanilla Pudding (see chapter on
    Basics)
1   10-ounce jar of strawberry or raspberry jam or preserves,
    sweetened only with fruit juice

2   boxes fresh strawberries, washed, hulled, drained and sliced
    (or 1 cup sliced almonds, toasted)

Prepare meringue shell according to instructions, and chill meringue in baking sheet in refrigerator. The meringue can be made the day before serving. Prepare double recipe of pudding, cool to room temperature before filling meringue. Chill until pudding is firmly set, then carefully spread on preserves and arrange sliced strawberries or almonds on top. Chill until ready to serve. Serves 12.

Giant Cherry Almond Party Meringue

This light dessert is for cherry lovers.

1   Giant Soft Meringue Party Shell (see chapter on Basics)
    double recipe of Cherry Pie Filling (see Index)
1   cup sliced almonds, toasted

Prepare meringue shell according to instructions, and chill meringue in baking sheet in refrigerator. The meringue can be made the day before serving.

Prepare a double recipe of Cherry Pie Filling. As soon as the filling is cool, gently spread it evenly over the meringue, leaving a 1-inch border. Sprinkle evenly with sliced almonds, and chill until serving. Serves 12.

Giant Blueberry Party Meringue

This light beautiful dessert can be topped with fresh blueberries in season.

    1   Giant Soft Meringue Party Shell (see chapter on Basics)
           double recipe of Blueberry Pie Filling (see Index)
1 or 2   boxes fresh blueberries in season, washed and well drained

Prepare meringue shell according to instructions, and chill meringue in baking sheet in refrigerator. The meringue can be made the day before serving.

Prepare double recipe of Blueberry Pie Filling. As soon as pie filling cools, gently spread filling all over meringue, leaving a 1-inch border. Sprinkle fresh blueberries on top and chill. Serves 12.

Giant Lemon Party Meringue

This light lemon meringue dessert is delicous.

    1   Giant Soft Meringue Party Shell (see chapter on Basics)
           double recipe of Lemon Pudding (see Index)

Prepare meringue shell according to instructions, and chill meringue in baking sheet in refrigerator. The meringue can be made the day before serving.

Prepare a double recipe of Lemon Pudding. As soon as pudding is room temperature, gently spread the pudding evenly over the meringue, leaving a 1-inch border. Chill until ready to serve. Serves 12.

Elegant Trifle

This beautiful dessert is deliciously layered with sponge cake, custard, jam and fresh sliced berries, and free of cholesterol.

   1/2   Orange Honey Sponge Cake (see chapter on Basics)
   1/3   cup orange juice
           double recipe of Flavorful Vanilla Pudding (see chapter on Basics)
   1/2   cup berry jam, fruit sweetened

    2   boxes fresh strawberries, washed, hulled, drained and sliced

Layer 1/2 of the sponge cake slices in the bottom of a decorative 3-quart glass bowl. Spoon 1/2 of the juice on top of cake slices, spread 1/2 of jam on top of cake layer, then 1/2 of the pudding over cake slices, and arrange 1/2 of the sliced berries on top. Repeat all these layers, ending with sliced strawberries on top. Chill well before serving. Serves 12.

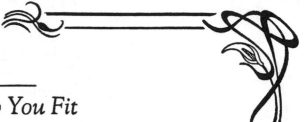

Chapter 5

Guilt-Free Pies to Keep You Fit

Imagine fruit pies, cheese pies, custard pies, pumpkin pies, tofu pies, and rice pudding, all made innocently with ingredients that are wholegrain, low-fat, low-salt, low-cholesterol, and sweetened only with fruit juices and honey.

Pie crusts are usually made with sugar, butter and white flour. Ours are made with wholegrain cereals and fruit juices. Some of our pies are crustless. Now you can enjoy pies to your heart's content, without feeling guilty, stuffed or deprived.

Apple Strudel Pie

This is a beautiful, light delicious dessert.

9 medium-size red or golden delicious apples

1 cup frozen concentrated apple juice
1 1/2 tablespoons lemon juice
1 tablespoon cinnamon
1/2 teaspoon coriander

2 cups wheat flakes or corn flakes
1/2 cup walnut chunks (optional)
3 tablespoons frozen concentrated apple juice
2 teaspoons cinnamon
1/2 teaspoon coriander

1 cup wheat flakes or corn flakes for crust

Cut peeled apples into quarters, remove core and seeds, and cut each quarter into 4 slices. In a 4 or 5-quart covered saucepan, cook the apple slices, with apple juice, lemon juice and spices for 12 minutes, covered, over medium heat. Remove lid and continue cooking apples for another 10 minutes, stirring occasionally. Remove apple slices with a slotted spoon to a large mixing bowl. Continue cooking the remaining liquid in the pan, uncovered for 8 minutes, or until it becomes syrupy. Add syrup to apple slices in the mixing bowl.

Coarsely chop cereal flakes and nuts in food processor or blender. In a small mixing bowl mix together the cereal flakes/nut mixture with the next 3 ingredients. Reserve 1 cup of this mixture for topping. Mix the remainder of this mixture with the apple slices.

To assemble pie arrange 1 cup of cereal flakes on the bottom of a 10-inch deep-dish glass oven-proof pie plate. Fill pie plate with the apple-cereal mixture, and sprinkle the reserved topping mixture on top. Cover pie with foil, pierce foil in 6 places, and bake pie in a 425-degree oven for 35 to 45 minutes. Remove foil and brown top of pie for an additional 10 minutes. Serves 6.

Lemon & Ginger Tofu Pie

This is an excellent, nutritious dessert with a delightful flavor.

2   16-ounce packages of soft-style tofu, drained and rinsed well
6   egg whites
       grated zest of 1 large lemon (lemon part of the peel)
3   tablespoons lemon juice
1/2   cup honey
1 1/2   tablespoons cornstarch or potato starch
2   teaspoons ginger

Blend all ingredients in a food processor or blender in batches. Pour mixture into a prepared Lemon-Ginger Crust, and bake pie in a 325-degree oven for 25 minutes. Chill before serving. Serves 6.

Lemon-Ginger Crust:
3/4   cup Fruit Sweetened Oat Bran Granola, coarsely chopped
          (see chapter on Basics), or commercial brand of granola
1   tablespoon frozen concentrated apple juice
1   tablespoon lemon juice
1   teaspoon ginger

In a 10-inch deep-dish glass oven-proof pie plate, mix all ingredients and pat mixture evenly on the bottom. Bake at 325-degrees for 10 to 12 minutes or until crust is set.

Apple & Cereal Casserole

This layered dessert casserole is so easy to prepare and such a wholesome treat. Apples can be sliced in a food processor and peel can be left on.

10   cups thinly sliced apples, peel left on
1   cup frozen concentrated apple juice
2   tablespoons cinnamon
1/2   teaspoon coriander
1   teaspoon lemon juice

4   cups wheat flakes or corn flakes

In a large mixing bowl toss first 5 ingredients. Arrange 1 1/2 cups of cereal flakes evenly on bottom of a 9x13-inch non-stick loaf pan. Then layer 1/2 of apple slices, 1 1/2 cups of cereal flakes, remaining 1/2 of apple slices, and remaining cup of cereal flakes on top. Spoon juice left in bowl over top, cover casserole with foil, and pierce foil in several places with a sharp knife to allow steam to escape.

Bake casserole at 425-degrees for 35 to 45 minutes or until apple slices are tender when pierced with a fork. Remove foil and continue to bake for 10 minutes longer. Remove and serve warm or cold. Serves 8.

Easy Apple & Cereal Bake

This easy-to-prepare dessert is a delicious and wholesome treat.

2	cups finely sliced delicious apples
2	tablespoons concentrated apple juice
2	teaspoons cinnamon
1/4	teaspoon coriander
1	cup raisin bran flakes or wheat flakes with raisins
1/4	cup walnut chunks (optional)

sprinkle of cinnamon for topping

In a large mixing bowl toss the first 6 ingredients together. Spread this mixture evenly in a 9x5-inch non-stick loaf pan. Sprinkle top with cinnamon. Cover with foil and pierce foil with sharp knife in 6 places. Bake in a 400-degree oven for 1 hour. Remove foil and continue baking for 10 minutes longer to brown. Remove and serve warm or cold as desired. Serves

Quick Apple & Raisin Bran Casserole

This delicious fruit sweetened apple dessert can be prepared quickly without peeling the apples or making a crust.

1 1/2	cups raisin-bran flakes
3	pounds of tart green apples, unpeeled, cored and thinly sliced (may be sliced in food processor)
1	cup frozen concentrated apple juice
2	tablespoons cinnamon
1/2	teaspoon coriander
2	tablespoons honey (optional)
1	cup raisin-bran flakes
1/2	cup chopped walnuts (optional)
3	tablespoons frozen concentrated apple juice
2	teaspoons cinnamon

sprinkle of cinnamon for top

Sprinkle 1 1/2 cups of raisin-bran flakes evenly in the bottom of a 9x13-inch glass oven-proof baking dish. Toss the next 5 ingredients in a large mixing bowl. Spread apple slices over cereal flakes, and spoon the remaining juice left in bowl over the apple slices.

Mix together the next 4 ingredients for topping, and sprinkle topping mixture evenly over the apple slices. Sprinkle generously with cinnamon, cover with foil, and pierce foil in 6 places with a sharp knife to allow steam to escape. Bake casserole in a 400-degree oven for 50 minutes. Remove foil and continue baking for 10 minutes longer, or until top of casserole is crusty and brown. Serves 10 to 12.

Banana Custard Pie

It's hard to imagine that a pie so low in fat and with no cholesterol can be so rich tasting, delicious and satisfying. You won't miss the cream and egg yolks one bit.

Walnut-Orange Cereal Crust:
- 1/2 cup raw walnuts
- 1 cup wheat flakes or corn flakes
- 1 tablespoon frozen concentrated orange juice
- 2 tablespoons cold water

- 1 tablespoon frozen concentrated orange juice

Coarsely chop first 4 ingredients in a blender or food processor until mixture holds together. Pat crust mixture in bottom of a 10-inch deep-dish glass oven-proof pie plate. Spread additional 1 tablespoon concentrated orange juice evenly on top of crust as a glaze. Bake crust in a 350-degree oven for 15 minutes or until crust is set and brown around edges. Remove crust from oven and cool.

Vanilla Custard Pie Filling:
- 1 cup non-fat milk
- 1/3 cup honey
- 1/3 cup dry non-fat milk powder

- 1 3/4 cups non-fat milk

- 1/4 cup cornstarch or potato starch
- 1/4 cup non-fat milk

- 1 tablespoon vanilla

Bring water in bottom of double boiler to a boil. Meanwhile blend the first 3 ingredients in a blender or food processor until smooth. Pour this mixture into the top of double boiler, and add remaining non-fat milk. Heat, stirring occasionally (about 20 minutes). Mix together cornstarch and milk until smooth, and gradually stir in this mixture. Cook for about 10 minutes longer, stirring occasionally. Stir in vanilla and cool for 10 minutes. Yields filling for 1 pie.

Banana Slices for Pie Filling and Decoration:
- 3 cups banana slices (3 to 4 bananas)
- 1 tablespoon lemon juice

- 1 large chilled banana, sliced, for decoration before serving

Toss banana slices in lemon juice and set aside.

To assemble pie: Once Vanilla Custard Pie Filling is ready, arrange 3 cups of the banana slices evenly on top of pie crust. Spread custard filling evenly on top of banana slices, and chill. Before serving, slice chilled banana and decorate top. Will serve 8.

Crustless Creamy Vanilla Custard Pie

Imagine a delicious creamy custard pie without cholesterol. This is the guilt-free one to be eaten and enjoyed to your heart's content.

9 egg whites
1/2 cup honey
3 tablespoons dry non-fat milk powder
3 tablespoons whole wheat pastry flour
1/4 teaspoon nutmeg
2 teaspoons vanilla

3 cups non-fat milk
generous sprinkle of nutmeg for top

Blend first 6 ingredients in a blender or food processor, in batches if necessary. Place mixture in a large mixing bowl, and stir in milk until blended. Pour custard mixture in a 10-inch deep-dish glass oven-proof pie plate and sprinkle top with nutmeg. Bake pie in a 325-degree oven for 40 minutes. Do not bake longer. Custard will set firmer as it chills. Serves 6.

Thanksgiving Pumpkin Pies

This recipe makes 2 divine tasting low-fat pumpkin pies that taste as good, or better, than those made with cream, sugar and whole eggs.

2 recipes Whole Wheat Low-Fat Pie Crust (see chapter on Basics)

3/4 cup honey
8 egg whites
1 29-ounce can of pumpkin puree

1 cup non-fat milk
3 tablespoons whole wheat flour
1/4 cup dry non-fat milk powder
2 teaspoons cinnamon
1 teaspoon ginger
1/2 teaspoon cloves

2 cups non-fat milk

Preheat oven to 425-degrees. In a large mixing bowl beat the honey and egg whites with a whisk until frothy. Whisk in pumpkin. Blend the next 6 ingredients in a blender or food processor, and add, all at once, mixing until smooth. Stir in milk and mix well. Pour mixture into 2 prepared unbaked Whole Wheat Low-Fat Pie Crusts. **Reduce oven temperature to 350-degrees** and bake for 45 to 50 minutes, or until filling is puffed, and knife in center comes out clean. Yields 2 pies, and serves 10 to 12.

Holiday French Apple Pie

What a treat to serve this pure wholesome and delicious pie on the holidays or on any festive occasion.

    2   cups wheat flakes or corn flakes
    1/4 cup frozen concentrated apple juice
    2   teaspoons cinnamon
    1/2 cup walnut chunks (optional)

    8   cups thinly sliced delicious apples, unpeeled. (Can be sliced in a food
         processor.)
    4   teaspoons cinnamon
    1/2 teaspoon coriander
    1/4 teaspoon cloves
    1/3 cup frozen concentrated apple juice
    1   teaspoon vanilla

Coarsely chop the first 4 ingredients in a blender or food processor. Spread 1/2 of this mixture in the bottom of a 10-inch deep-dish glass oven-proof pie plate. In a large mixing bowl mix together apple slices, spices, apple juice and vanilla. Fill pie plate with apple slices, pour any juice left in bowl, and then sprinkle the cereal flake mixture evenly on top.

Cover the pie with foil, and pierce foil in 6 places. Bake in a 400-degree oven for 50 to 60 minutes or until apples are tender. Uncover pie and let it brown for 10 minutes longer. Serve warm or cold. Serves 6.

Quick and Easy Apple Pie

This healthy and delicious pie takes only minutes to assemble. Serve warm or cold.

    1   cup wheat flakes or corn flakes, coarsely chopped

    6   large Delicious apples, unpeeled, sliced thin. (Can be sliced in a food
         processor.)
    1   6-ounce can frozen concentrated apple juice
    1   teaspoon lemon juice
    1   tablespoon cinnamon

         sprinkle of cinnamon for top

Sprinkle crumbled cereal flakes in the bottom of a 10-inch deep-dish glass oven-proof pie plate. Mix together next 4 ingredients in a large bowl. Spread apple mixture over cereal in pie plate and pour juice left in bowl over the apple slices. Sprinkle with cinnamon. Cover pie tightly with foil. Pierce foil with a sharp knife in several places to allow steam to escape and bake in a 400-degree oven for approximately 40 to 45 minutes or until apples are tender. Remove foil and allow pie to brown for 10 to 15 minutes longer. Serves 6.

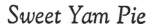

Sweet Yam Pie

This pie is excellent. Besides being simply delicious it is also so good for you. If you would like to add a crust, use Whole Wheat Low-Fat Pie Crust (see chapter on Basics.)

2	cups cooked yams, peeled, solidly packed down (about 2 pounds)
1/2	cup non-fat milk
3	tablespoons dry non-fat milk powder
2	tablespoons whole wheat flour
1/4	cup honey
1 1/2	teaspoons cinnamon
3/4	teaspoon ginger
1/4	teaspoon cloves
1	cup non-fat milk
6	egg whites
	sprinkle of cinnamon for top

Preheat oven to 425-degrees. In a food processor or blender puree the yams and next 3 ingredients, in batches if necessary. Set aside. In a large mixing bowl stir in next 6 ingredients and beat well with a whisk. Stir in yam mixture well until blended. Spread mixture into a 10-inch deep-dish glass oven-proof pie plate. Bake in a 425-degree oven for 20 minutes, then **reduce oven temperature to 350-degrees,** and bake pie for an additional 20 minutes longer, or until filling is set. Serves 6.

Crustless Pineapple & Honey Cheese Pie

This delicious low-cholesterol treat takes only minutes to prepare. It is innocently sweetened with pineapple juice and a little honey.

3	cups low-fat cottage cheese
1/2	cup frozen concentrated pineapple juice
5	tablespoons honey
6	egg whites
1/4	teaspoon almond extract
1/2	teaspoon vanilla
3	tablespoons potato starch
1	cup crushed pineapple, unsweetened, well drained

Whip cottage cheese in blender or food processor until smooth and creamy. Set aside. In a large mixing bowl, beat next 6 ingredients, with a whisk, until blended and frothy. Whisk in whipped cottage cheese. Pour cheese mixture into a 10-inch deep-dish glass oven-proof pie plate, and bake pie in a 325-degree oven for 25 minutes. Do not bake longer. Cheese filling will set as it chills. Spoon crushed pineapple on top of each serving. Serves 6.

Blueberry Pie

This healthy pie is both delicious and beautiful to look at. If a double crusted pie is preferred, follow instructions in Cherry Pie recipe.

- 1   double recipe of Whole Wheat Low-Fat Pie Crust
  (see chapter on Basics)
- 1/2   teaspoon oil for pan

- 1   egg white
- 1   tablespoon honey

Blueberry Pie Filling:
- 6   cups frozen blueberries, or fresh berries
- 1/2   cup frozen concentrated apple juice
- 1/4   cup frozen concentrated orange juice
- 1/4   cup honey
- 1/4   cup whole wheat flour
- 2   tablespoons cornstarch or potato starch

Preheat oven to 450-degrees. Prepare double recipe of Whole Wheat Low-Fat Pie Crust according to instructions. Divide dough in half, and roll out lower crust into an 11-inch circle between 2 pieces of wax paper. Oil the bottom and sides of a 10-inch deep-dish glass oven-proof pie plate, and fit crust into the pie plate. Mix together egg white and honey and brush the bottom crust with this mixture. Reserve remainder of this mixture for glazing the top crust. Pierce bottom crust in several places with a sharp knife, and bake lower crust in a 450-degree oven for 7 minutes. Meanwhile roll out the other half of the pie dough between 2 sheets of wax paper and set it aside.

In a 4 to 5-quart non-stick saucepan mix together next 6 ingredients, and cook mixture over medium heat, stirring frequently until mixture thickens. Stir berries gently to keep them whole. Remove from heat and spread hot blueberry mixture evenly into bottom crust. To prepare lattice work for top of pie remove upper sheet of wax paper from rolled out pie dough. Cut the circular crust into strips, slightly less than 1/2-inch thick. Arrange 5 strips of dough in one direction, and 4 or 5 strips of dough in the other direction forming a lattice pattern. Arrange remaining strips of dough around outer edge of pie to hold strips down. With a fork make design all around the outer edge. Brush lattice work and outer Blueberry Pie Crust with honey-egg white glaze, and bake pie for 10 minutes in a 450-degree oven. Reduce oven temperature to 350-degrees, and continue baking pie for another 30 minutes. Serves 6.

Boysenberry Pie

Boysenberry lovers will enjoy this tasty, delicious pie.

- 1 double recipe of Whole Wheat Low-Fat Pie Crust
  (see chapter on Basics)
- 1/2 teaspoon oil for pan

- 1 egg white
- 1 tablespoon honey

Boysenberry Pie Filling:
- 6 cups frozen boysenberries, unthawed, or fresh berries
- 3/4 cup frozen concentrated apple juice
- 1/4 cup honey
- 1/4 cup whole wheat flour
- 2 tablespoons cornstarch or potato starch

Follow directions for preparing the crust in Blueberry Pie (preceding recipe). In a large non-stick pan mix together the boysenberries, apple juice concentrate, honey, flour and cornstarch or potato starch. Stir frequently until mixture thickens. Remove filling from heat and spread mixture evenly in prepared crust. Continue following Blueberry Pie recipe for preparing lattice top crust and baking instructions. Serves 6.

Divine Baked Apples

The aroma of these apples baking is a real treat. We enjoy them for breakfast, dessert or snacks. They are healthy and so easy to prepare.

- 4 large Roman Beauty apples, cores removed, leaving 1/2-inch base
  of core intact

- 1 teaspoon cinnamon
- 4 whole cloves
  sprinkle of coriander
- 8 teaspoons frozen concentrated pineapple juice

- 1 cup water
- 1 teaspoon cinnamon
- 2 whole cloves
- 2 tablespoons frozen concentrated pineapple juice
- 1/4 cup black raisins

Place cored apples in a 10-inch deep-dish glass oven-proof pie plate. Fill hole in each apple with 1/4 teaspoon cinnamon, one clove, a dash of coriander and 2 teaspoons concentrated pineapple juice. Pour water, spices, and pineapple juice concentrate around apples, and add raisins. Bake in 350-degree oven for approximately 1 1/2 hours or until apples are brown and soft to touch. Remove from oven and baste with its own juice. Remove cloves and store in refrigerator. Serves 4.

Strawberry Custard Trifle Pie

This delicious dessert can be assembled quickly once the sponge cake and custard pudding is ready. The sponge cake and custard can be made well ahead of time.

    1/4   Orange Honey Sponge Cake (see chapter on Basics)
    1/4   cup orange juice
    1/2   recipe Flavorful Vanilla Pudding (see chapter on Basics)

    1/4   cup berry jam, fruit sweetened

    1   box fresh strawberries, washed, hulled, drained and sliced

Cut the sponge cake into 1/2-inch slices and layer cake slices in bottom of a 10-inch deep-dish glass pie plate. Spoon orange juice over cake slices and spread cold pudding on top of cake slices. With a spoon spread jam evenly over pudding layer and arrange sliced strawberries attractively on top. Chill pie until ready to serve. Serves 6.

Strawberry & Rhubarb Cobbler

This is a delightfully tart dessert with a crunchy topping. The strawberries and rhubarb complement each other perfectly.

    1   20-ounce package frozen strawberries, unsweetened
    1   20-ounce package frozen cut rhubarb, unsweetened
    1/3   cup honey
    2/3   cup apple juice
    1/4   cup whole wheat flour
    2   tablespoons cornstarch or potato starch

It is not necessary to thaw strawberries and rhubarb. Mix all ingredients together in a large non-stick pot and stir frequently until mixture thickens. (This will not become very thick.) Spread fruit mixture in a 9x9-inch glass oven-proof baking dish. Then prepare topping.

Topping:
    1/2   cup rolled oats
    1/2   cup chopped pecans (optional)
    2   teaspoons cinnamon
    3   tablespoons frozen concentrated apple juice
    1   tablespoon oil

In a medium size mixing bowl mix together all of the topping ingredients, stirring well with a fork. Sprinkle the topping evenly on top of the strawberry and rhubarb layer, and bake cobbler in a 375-degree oven for 30 to 40 minutes or until topping is brown and crunchy. Serve warm or cold as desired. Serves 8.

Baked Brown Rice Pudding

This wholesome, low-fat rice pudding is delicious for breakfast or snacks.

6	egg whites
1 2/3	cups non-fat milk
4	tablespoons dry non-fat milk powder
1	tablespoon cinnamon
1	teaspoon coriander
1 1/3	cups frozen concentrated apple juice
1	tablespoon vanilla
2	tablespoons whole wheat flour
3	cups cooked brown rice
1	cup black raisins
1/2	cup walnut chunks (optional)
	generous sprinkle of nutmeg for top

In a large bowl, whisk together the first 8 ingredients until smooth and frothy. Stir in rice and raisins. Pour mixture into a 9x13-inch glass oven-proof baking dish, and sprinkle nuts and nutmeg on top. Bake in a 375-degree oven for 30 to 35 minutes, or until set and slightly puffed around edges. Do not overbake. Serves 10 to 12.

Apple Spice Cheese Pie

This lovely flavored low-cholesterol cheese pie is a real treat.

3	cups low-fat cottage cheese
1/2	cup frozen concentrated apple juice
1/4	cup honey
1	teaspoon cinnamon
1/2	teaspoon nutmeg
1	teaspoon vanilla
1	tablespoon cornstarch or potato starch
2	tablespoons whole wheat pastry flour
6	egg whites

Whip cottage cheese in a food processor until smooth, then place in a large bowl. In the food processor bowl blend remaining ingredients for 30 seconds. Stir this mixture into the whipped cottage cheese. Pour cheesecake mixture into prepared Wholegrain Cereal Crust and bake in a 325-degree oven for 30 minutes. Do not overbake. Serves 6.

Wholegrain Cereal Crust:

3/4	cup wheat flakes or corn flakes
2	tablespoons frozen concentrated apple juice
1	teaspoon cinnamon
1/2	teaspoon nutmeg

In a blender or food processor coarsely chop the cereal flakes with remaining crust ingredients. Spread mixture evenly in the bottom of a 10-inch deep-dish glass oven-proof pie plate, and pat it down with finger tips. Bake crust in a 325-degree oven for 10 minutes or just until crust is set.

Apple Custard Casserole

This recipe is a true delight to look at, to serve, and to eat.

- 3 cups wheat flakes or corn flakes
- 8 cups Delicious apples, peeled, cored and sliced. (Can be sliced in a food processor.)
- 6 ounces concentrated frozen apple juice
- 1/2 teaspoon coriander
- 2 teaspoons cinnamon

- 1 cup non-fat milk
- 6 tablespoons dry non-fat milk powder
- 6 egg whites
- 1/3 cup honey
- 2 tablespoons whole wheat flour
- 1 teaspoon vanilla
- 1/4 teaspoon nutmeg

- 1 2/3 cups non-fat milk
  generous sprinkle of nutmeg for top

Coarsely chop cereal flakes in blender or food processor, and sprinkle on bottom of a 9x13-inch non-stick or glass oven-proof baking dish. Mix together apple slices, apple juice and spices in a large mixing bowl. Spread apple slices over cereal in baking pan and pour any juice left in bowl over the apple slices. Cover with foil and pierce foil with a sharp knife in 8 to 10 places as you would pierce a pie crust. Bake covered in 400-degree oven for 25 minutes, then uncovered for 10 minutes.

Meanwhile blend the next 7 ingredients in a blender or food processor until smooth. Pour custard mixture into a large mixing bowl. Stir in milk and mix well. Remove apple casserole from oven and pour custard over the hot baked apple slices. Top with nutmeg. Reduce oven temperature to 350-degrees and continue baking casserole uncovered for 12 to 15 minutes or until custard is set. Do not bake longer. Custard will set as it chills. Serves 12.

Cherry Pie

This easy-to-prepare fruit-sweetened double-crusted pie is a delicious wholesome treat.

- 1 double recipe of Whole Wheat Low-Fat Pie Crust (see Basics)
- 1 egg white
- 1 tablespoon frozen concentrated orange juice

Cherry Pie Filling:
- 6 cups frozen dark sweet pitted cherries
- 1/2 cup frozen concentrated apple juice
- 2 tablespoons honey
- 1 tablespoon lemon juice
- 1/4 cup water
- 1/4 cup whole wheat flour
- 2 tablespoons cornstarch or potato starch
  grated zest of 1 orange (orange part of the peel)

(Continued)

(Cherry Pie, Cont.)

Preheat oven to 450-degrees. Prepare double recipe of Whole Wheat Low-Fat Pie Crust according to instructions. Divide dough in half, and roll out lower crust into an 11-inch circle between 2 pieces of wax paper. Lightly oil the bottom and sides of a 10-inch deep-dish glass oven-proof pie plate, and fit crust into the pie plate. Mix together egg white and orange juice and brush the bottom with this mixture. (Reserve remainder of this mixture for glazing the top.) Pierce bottom in several places with a sharp knife, and bake in a 450-degree oven for 7 minutes. Meanwhile, roll out the other half of the pie dough between 2 sheets of wax paper and set it aside.

In a 4 to 5-quart non-stick saucepan, mix together the next 8 ingredients, and cook over medium heat, stirring frequently until mixture thickens. Remove from heat and spread this hot cherry mixture into bottom crust. Remove upper piece of wax paper from top crust and turn crust over on top of cherries, fold under any extra crust and flute edges with fingers. Brush upper crust with the orange juice-egg white mixture. Bake pie in a 450-degree oven for 10 minutes then reduce oven temperature to 350-degrees. Continue baking pie for an additional 30 minutes, or until top is deep golden brown. Serves 6.

Cholesterol-Free Crustless Lemon Meringue Pudding Pie

Imagine being able to prepare a beautiful, innocent lemon meringue pie without egg yolks and sugar. This one will give you and your loved ones even more pleasure, knowing that it's healthy for you.

Lemon Pudding:
- 3 egg whites
- 1/4 cup fresh lemon juice
- grated zest of 1 lemon (yellow part of the peel)
- 1 tablespoon oil

- 3/4 cup cold water
- 1/4 cup cornstarch or potato starch
- 1/3 cup frozen concentrated orange juice
- 1/3 cup honey

Whip egg whites until stiff but not dry and set aside. Mix together lemon juice, rind and oil and set aside.

In a 2-quart non-stick saucepan bring the last 4 ingredients to a boil, stirring constantly until pudding thickens. Immediately stir in whipped egg whites and stir constantly for 1 minute longer. Remove pudding from stove and stir in lemon juice, grated rind and oil. Pour pudding immediately into a 10-inch deep-dish glass oven-proof pie plate, and allow pudding to cool. Then prepare meringue topping.

Meringue Topping:
- 6 egg whites
- 1/2 teaspoon cream of tartar
- 1/4 cup honey

(Continued)

(Lemon Meringue Pudding Pie, Cont.)

Preheat oven to 400-degrees. In the large bowl of an electric mixer, beat egg whites and cream of tartar until foamy, then gradually beat in honey. Continue to beat whites until soft peaks form. Gently spread meringue on top of lemon pudding, beginning along outer edges and mounding meringue highest in center. Bake for 7 to 9 minutes or until golden. Cool, then chill well in refrigerator before serving. Serves 6.

Creamy Cheese Pie

This delicately lemon-flavored cheese pie has no cream cheese, but it tastes creamy and delicious without it.

Lemon Cereal Flakes Crust:
- 1   cup wheat flakes or corn flakes
- 1   tablespoon lemon juice
- 2   tablespoons honey

Coarsely chop cereal flakes with lemon juice and honey in a blender or food processor. Spread mixture evenly in a 10-inch deep-dish glass oven-proof pie plate. Bake crust at 350-degrees for 10 minutes or until set and light brown.

Creamy Cheese Filling:
- 3   cups low-fat cottage cheese
- 6   egg whites
- 1   tablespoon plain non-fat or low-fat yogurt
- 1   tablespoon lemon juice
- 2/3 cup honey
- 3   tablespoons cornstarch or potato starch
- 1   teaspoon vanilla
      grated rind of 1/2 lemon

In a food processor blend the cottage cheese until creamy and place in a mixing bowl. Next blend remaining 7 ingredients in food processor until smooth, and add to whipped cottage cheese, mixing together thoroughly. Pour pie filling into a prepared Lemon Cereal Flakes Crust and bake pie in a 350-degree oven for 25 to 30 minutes. Do not overbake. Meanwhile prepare Honey Lemon Yogurt Topping.

Honey Lemon Yogurt Topping:
- 1   cup non-fat or low-fat yogurt
- 2   tablespoons honey
- 1   teaspoon lemon juice
- 1   tablespoon cornstarch or potato starch

Mix together topping ingredients until smooth. Remove cheese pie from oven, spread yogurt topping evenly on top, return pie to oven, and bake pie in a 350-degree oven for 8 to 10 minutes longer. Cool and then chill pie well before serving. Serves 6.

Carob & Mocha Pudding Pie

Imagine yourself enjoying a big piece of this luscious rich-tasting pudding pie without any cholesterol. This crustless pie is absolutely guilt-free.

Carob Mocha Pudding:
- 4 tablespoons carob powder
- 2 teaspoons instant coffee substitute
- 4 tablespoons non-fat milk powder
- 1/2 cup boiling water

- 1/3 cup honey
- 1 teaspoon dark molasses
- 2 3/4 cups non-fat milk
- 1/4 cup cornstarch or potato starch
- 1/4 cup cold non-fat milk
- 2 teaspoons vanilla

In the top of the double boiler, over simmering water, mix together the first 4 ingredients until smooth. Stir in honey and molasses, then milk. If this mixture is lumpy, strain or puree until smooth. Cook mixture for 20 minutes, stirring occasionally. Mix together cornstarch or potato starch, milk and vanilla, and gradually stir into pudding mixture. Continue cooking pudding for 10 minutes longer, stirring occasionally until pudding thickens. Immediately pour pudding into a 10-inch deep-dish glass oven-proof pie plate and set aside while preparing meringue topping.

Carob Meringue Topping:
- 6 egg whites
- 1/4 teaspoon cream of tartar
- 4 tablespoons honey
- 1 tablespoon carob powder

Preheat oven to 400-degrees. In a small bowl of an electric mixer beat egg whites with cream of tartar until foamy. Add honey and carob powder, and continue to beat whites until stiff and glossy. Gently spread meringue topping over the pudding in pie plate, sealing outer edges first, then spreading evenly over entire top of pie. Bake meringue in a 400-degree oven for 7 to 9 minutes, or until golden. Cool, then chill pie well before serving. Serves 6.

Chapter 6

Chewy Wholegrain Cookies and Snacks

Most cookies and snacks are made with white flour, sugar, butter, margarine, hydrogenated fat, whole eggs, and salt. Ours are made with wholegrain flour and cereal, and the purest, wholesome and nutritious ingredients, low in fat, cholesterol, salt, and without sugar.

You can think of our cookies and snacks as good food to be eaten and enjoyed. Now instead of feeling guilty, you can feel assured you are eating nutritious food, fiber and vitamins your body needs each day.

Please store the cookies and snacks made from our recipes in the refrigerator or freezer until ready to be eaten. This will protect their natural, wholesome goodness. Before serving, cookies can be crisped in a 350° oven for 3 to 5 minutes, or in a toaster oven for 1 minute.

Fruit Sweetened Carob Brownies

These moist, wholegrain, low-fat brownies are so delicious they are sure to be a favorite of yours as they are ours. For added lusciousness, frost with Date Carob Fudge Frosting before cutting into squares.

1 1/2	cups pitted dates, solidly packed
1	cup black raisins
1 1/2	cups boiling water
3/4	cup carob powder
1/2	cup non-fat or low-fat yogurt
4	egg whites
2	teaspoons vanilla
1	tablespoon oil
2	teaspoons dark molasses
1 1/2	cups whole wheat pastry flour
2	teaspoons baking soda
3/4	cup walnut pieces (optional)

In a small non-stick saucepan cook the dates and raisins in boiling water for 5 minutes. Remove pan from stove and stir in carob powder. Puree this mixture in a food processor or blender, and place this mixture in a large mixing bowl. Add the next 5 ingredients and beat well. Mix together the flour and baking soda, and add all at once, mixing just until smooth. Fold in nuts. Spread the batter in a 10x15-inch non-stick jelly roll pan, and bake in a 400-degree oven for 10 to 12 minutes. Do not overbake. Cool and cut into 2x3-inch bars. Yields 25 brownies.

Banana Oat Bran Raisin Cookies

These fruit flavored cookies make a lean, healthy snack, high in natural fiber and wholegrain goodness.

1 1/3	cups pureed bananas (about 3 medium bananas)
2/3	cup frozen concentrated apple juice
4	egg whites
2	teaspoons vanilla
1	tablespoon oil
2/3	cup whole wheat flour
2	teaspoons baking powder
1 1/2	tablespoons cinnamon
1 1/2	cups oat bran
1	cup black raisins
	sprinkle of cinnamon for top

In a large mixing bowl, whisk together first 5 ingredients until blended. Mix together the flour, baking powder, and cinnamon, and add, all at once, mixing only until smooth. Fold in oat bran and raisins. Drop cookie dough on a non-stick cookie sheet, forming 12 extra large cookies. Sprinkle generously with cinnamon, and bake cookies in a 400-degree oven for 30 minutes, or until golden brown. Yields 12 cookies.

Spicy Gingerbread Bars

These innocent, low-fat gingerbread bars are made with spices and whole wheat flour.

1	12-ounce package frozen cooked orange-colored squash, thawed
2	egg whites
1	tablespoon oil
3/4	cup hot water
1/2	cup dark molasses
2 1/4	cups whole wheat flour
1 1/2	teaspoons baking powder
1/2	teaspoon baking soda
1	teaspoon ginger
1	teaspoon cinnamon
1/2	teaspoon cloves

In a large mixing bowl, whisk together first 5 ingredients until blended. Mix together the flour, baking powder, baking soda and spices, and add, all at once, mixing only until smooth. Do not overmix. Spread batter evenly in a 9x9-inch non-stick baking pan, and bake in a 350-degree oven for 45 to 50 minutes, or until gingerbread tastes done. Allow it to cool before cutting into 1x3-inch bars. Yields 27 cookies.

Spicy Oat Bran Cereal Bars

These easy-to-prepare bars, made with oat bran flakes cereal, are full of fiber and flavor. We keep them in the freezer to enjoy at any time.

1/2	cup frozen concentrated apple juice, thawed
2	egg whites
1	tablespoon oil
2	tablespoons honey

1/2	cup whole wheat flour
1	teaspoon baking soda
1	tablespoon cinnamon
1	tablespoon nutmeg

1/2	cup black raisins
4	cups oat bran flakes

In a large mixing bowl whisk together first 4 ingredients until blended. Mix together flour, baking soda and spices, and add, all at once, mixing only until smooth. Stir in raisins and fold in oat bran flakes. Press mixture in a 9x13-inch non-stick baking pan. Bake for 20 to 25 minutes in a 400-degree oven or until brown on top. Cut into bars when cool. Yields 24 to 30 bars.

Fudge Carob Cookies

These light delicious fruit-sweetened cookies are low-fat and guilt-free.

1/2	cup pitted dates
1/2	cup black raisins
1/2	cup water

1/2	cup carob powder

1/3	cup non-fat or low-fat yogurt
3	egg whites
1	teaspoon vanilla
1	tablespoon oil
1 1/2	teaspoons dark molasses

3/4	cup whole wheat flour
1	teaspoon baking soda
1/3	cup walnut pieces (optional)

In a small, non-stick saucepan bring dates, raisins and water to a boil, and cook for 1 minute. Remove pan from heat, and stir in carob powder. Blend date mixture, along with the next 5 ingredients, in a food processor or blender. Place this mixture into a large mixing bowl. Mix together flour and baking soda, and add all at once, stirring only until smooth. Fold in walnuts. Spoon heaping tablespoons of batter on a non-stick cookie sheet and bake at 400-degrees for 10 to 12 minutes. Yields 18 cookies.

Quick Pineapple Oatmeal Cookies

In just minutes you can enjoy these delicious wholesome wholegrain fruit-sweetened cookies.

1/2	cup frozen concentrated pineapple juice
1/2	cup buttermilk
1	teaspoon oil
1	teaspoon vanilla
2	egg whites
1	cup whole wheat flour
2	teaspoons baking soda
1 1/2	tablespoons cinnamon
1	cup rolled oats
1/2	cup black raisins
1/2	cup chopped walnuts (optional)

In a large mixing bowl, whisk together first 5 ingredients until blended. Mix together the flour, baking soda and cinnamon, and add, all at once, mixing just until smooth. Do not overmix. Fold in oats, raisins and walnuts. On a non-stick cookie sheet drop the cookie batter, forming 12 large cookies. Bake in a 425-degree oven for 12 minutes. Yields 12 cookies.

Yam & Oat Bran Spice Cookies

These fruit and yam sweetened cookies are full of spicy wholegrain goodness and oat bran.

1 1/4	cups baked or cooked yams, mashed (about 1 1/4 pounds)
2/3	cup frozen concentrated apple juice
4	egg whites
1	teaspoon vanilla
1	tablespoon oil
2/3	cup whole wheat flour
2	teaspoons baking powder
1	cup oat bran
1	tablespoon cinnamon
1/2	teaspoon nutmeg
1 1/2	teaspoons ginger
1/4	teaspoon cloves
3/4	cup black raisins

In a large mixing bowl, whisk together the yams, apple juice, egg whites, vanilla and oil until blended. Mix together the next 7 ingredients, and add 1/2 of this mixture, mixing only until smooth. Fold in last half of dry ingredients and raisins. On a non-stick cookie sheet, shape cookie dough into large cookies, and bake them in a 375-degree oven for about 25 minutes or until cookies are brown. Yields 16 to 18 cookies.

Quick Carob Oatmeal Cookies

You can whip up these delicious "guilt-free" cookies in minutes. They are made with the most wholesome of ingredients to keep the body healthy and fit.

2	tablespoons non-fat milk
2	egg whites
1	tablespoon dark molasses
1/3	cup honey
1/2	cup non-fat or low-fat yogurt
1	tablespoon oil
2	teaspoons vanilla
3/4	cup whole wheat flour
1/4	cup carob powder
2	teaspoons baking soda
1	cup rolled oats
1/2	cup black raisins
2	tablespoons raw sunflower seeds (optional)

In a medium-size mixing bowl, whisk together first 7 ingredients until blended. Mix together flour, carob powder and baking soda, and add, all at once, mixing only until smooth. Stir in oats, raisins and sunflower seeds. Drop by rounded tablespoons on a non-stick cookie sheet. Allow space between cookies since these cookies spread out. Bake in a 400-degree oven for 8 to 10 minutes, or just until cookies are firm on top. Do not overbake. Yields 18 cookies.

Quick Orange Oatmeal Cookies

These crunchy, easy-to-prepare fruit sweetened cookies make great healthy wholegrain snacks.

2	egg whites
1/2	cup frozen concentrated orange juice
2	heaping tablespoons fruit sweetened orange marmalade
1	tablespoon oil
2	tablespoons water
1	cup whole wheat flour
2	teaspoons baking powder
1	cup rolled oats
1/2	cup black raisins
2	tablespoons raw sunflower seeds

In a medium-size mixing bowl, whisk together the first 5 ingredients. Mix together flour and baking powder, and add, all at once, mixing just until moistened. Fold in oats, raisins and sunflower seeds. Drop by rounded teaspoonfuls on a non-stick cookie sheet, and bake in a 400-degree oven for 15 to 18 minutes, or until cookies are brown. Yields 30 cookies.

Luscious Light Date Nut Cookies

These beautiful, light and healthy cookies are especially delicious.

1	cup pecan chunks

1 1/2	cups pitted dates
3	egg whites

6	egg whites
1/2	teaspoon cream of tartar

3	tablespoons honey
1 1/2	teaspoons vanilla

1 1/2	teaspoons cinnamon
2/3	cup whole wheat flour
1	teaspoon baking powder

Chop pecans in a blender or food processor. Blend in dates and 3 egg whites until dates are well mashed. Place date mixture in a large mixing bowl and set aside.

Beat 6 egg whites and cream of tartar in an electric mixer until foamy. Gradually beat in honey and vanilla and continue beating until whites are thick and shiny. Mix together cinnamon, flour and baking powder. Reduce speed and lightly fold dry ingredients into whites. Stir 1/2 of the egg white mixture into the date mixture, then carefully fold in the remaining egg white mixture.

Drop rounded teaspoonfuls on two non-stick cookie sheets, and bake in a 350-degree oven for approximately 20 minutes or until light brown. Yields 48 cookies.

Granola Maple Cookies

These crunchy cookies are innocent, wholesome treats and good to keep on hand in your refrigerator or freezer.

1	cup pitted dates
6	egg whites
1/4	cup maple syrup
1	teaspoon vanilla
1/2	cup whole wheat flour
4	cups Fruit Sweetened Oat Bran Granola (see chapter on Basics), or commercial brand

Puree first 5 ingredients in a food processor or blender. Place mixture into a large mixing bowl. Fold in granola just until blended. Place rounded teaspoons of cookie dough on two non-stick cookie sheets, and bake cookies in a 350-degree oven for 20 minutes or until brown. Yields 4 dozen cookies.

Spicy Yam Cereal Bars

These healthy, delicious treats are made with whole wheat flour and are spicy and wonderful. Who needs rich, sugary sweets, when these taste so good.

1	cup wheat flakes or corn flakes, coarsely chopped
1 1/2	teaspoons cinnamon
1 1/2	cups baked yams, peeled and mashed, (about 1 1/2 pounds)
3/4	cup frozen concentrated apple juice
1/4	cup frozen concentrated orange juice
6	egg whites
1	tablespoon cinnamon
1	teaspoon each, ginger, nutmeg and coriander
1/4	teaspoon ground cloves
1	cup whole wheat flour
1	teaspoon baking soda
1	teaspoon baking powder
2	cups rolled oats
1	cup raisins
1	cup chopped walnuts (optional)

Mix together cinnamon and cereal flakes. Spread mixture evenly on the bottom of a 10x15-inch non-stick jelly roll pan. In a large bowl beat yams, fruit juices, egg whites, and spices with a whisk. Mix together the flour, baking soda and baking powder and add, beating just until blended. Stir in oats, raisins and walnuts.

To spread the yam mixture on top of cereal crumbs in the jelly roll pan, drop batter by tablespoonfuls on top of the cereal; then spread gently to cover entire pan. Bake in a 350-degree oven for about 35 minutes or until top is firm to the touch and light brown in color. Allow to cool, then cut into squares with a plastic spatula. Store in refrigerator or freezer. Yields 36 to 48 bars.

Crunchy Honey Molasses Popcorn

For a special treat on some TV evening try this sweet crunchy popcorn.

1/2	cup honey
1/2	cup dark molasses
1 1/2	teaspoon oil
4	quarts popcorn, air popped preferred

In a medium-sized non-stick saucepan, boil the first 3 ingredients over medium heat until it reaches the hard ball stage, 260-degrees. Remove syrup from stove. In a large mixing bowl, place popcorn and carefully and slowly pour the hot syrup over the popcorn while stirring constantly with a wooden spoon. Be very careful, the syrup is hot. Yields 4 quarts.

Spicy Yam Cereal & Oat Bran Chews

It is so satisfying to munch on these healthy chews. Your family and friends will love them.

1 1/2	cups baked yams, peeled and mashed, (about 1 1/2 pounds)
4	egg whites
1/2	cup frozen concentrated apple juice
2	tablespoons frozen concentrated orange juice
1	teaspoon vanilla
1	cup whole wheat flour
1	teaspoon baking powder
1	tablespoon cinnamon
1	teaspoon nutmeg
1	teaspoon ginger
1	teaspoon coriander
1/4	teaspoon ground cloves
1	cup rolled oats
1 1/2	cups oat bran
1	cup black raisins

In a large mixing bowl whisk first 5 ingredients until frothy. Mix together flour, baking powder and spices, and add, all at once, whisking just until smooth. Stir in oats, oat bran and raisins.

Drop cookie dough by rounded teaspoons on 2 non-stick cookie sheets. Flatten cookies by pressing them with a fork. Bake in a 350-degree oven for about 20 minutes or until cookies are brown. Yields 48 cookies.

Puffed Wheat Carmel Crisps

These are for folks who enjoy crispy, healthy treats. They can be prepared quickly and stored in an airtight container or in the freezer.

1/2	cup dark molasses
2	tablespoons water
1/4	teaspoon ginger
1/2	teaspoon cinnamon
6	cups puffed wheat cereal (without salt, sugar or oil)

Boil molasses, water and spices in a large non-stick saucepan until it foams and rises. This will take only a few minutes. Quickly stir in puffed wheat cereal. When cereal is coated, spread mixture evenly into a 9x13-inch non-stick pan and bake in a 350-degree oven for 15 minutes or until crispy. Remove from oven and press down slightly with spatula. When cool break into pieces. Yields 15 cookies.

Onion Rye Oat Bran Cookies

If you like onions, this is a tasty way to enjoy oat bran.

        6   egg whites
        1   cup chopped onion, solidly packed down
        1   tablespoon molasses
      1/4   cup honey
        1   tablespoon oil
        2   tablespoons caraway seeds
        2   tablespoons sesame seeds

        1   cup rye flour
        2   cups oat bran
    1 1/2   teaspoons baking powder

In a large mixing bowl, whisk together first 7 ingredients. Mix together the flour, oat bran and baking powder, and add, all at once, mixing only until smooth. Do not overmix.

Drop from heaping tablespoons on a non-stick cookie sheet and press down with fork to form cookies 2 inches in diameter. Bake in a 400-degree oven for about 15 minutes. Do not overbake. Store in refrigerator or freezer. Yields 36 cookies.

Fruit Oat Bran Balls

These healthy, fruit-sweetened cookies are great tasting.

        1   cup rolled oats
    1 1/4   cups oat bran

      1/2   cup pitted dates
      1/2   cup raisins
        2   egg whites

      1/4   cup non-fat milk
        1   tablespoon frozen concentrated orange juice
        1   teaspoon vanilla
        1   teaspoon cinnamon
        1   tablespoon oil
             sprinkle of cinnamon for top

Toast oats and oat bran in a 400-degree oven in a non-stick cookie sheet for 8 to 10 minutes or until light brown. Meanwhile mash dates, raisins and egg whites in a blender or food processor. Place this mixture into a mixing bowl. Stir in next 5 ingredients and mix well, then stir in oats and oat bran. With moistened hands, form into small balls the size of walnuts. Place balls on a non-stick cookie sheet. They can be placed close together since they do not rise. Sprinkle with cinnamon, and bake in a 400-degree oven for 10 to 15 minutes or until light brown. Yields approximately 50 balls.

Pumpkin Spice Oat Bran Chews

These cookies are so healthy, they make a wholesome easy breakfast. We keep a tin of them handy in our freezer.

1 1/2	cups canned pumpkin puree
4	egg whites
2/3	cup honey
1	teaspoon vanilla
1	cup whole wheat flour
1	teaspoon baking powder
1	tablespoon cinnamon
1	teaspoon nutmeg
1	teaspoon ginger
1	teaspoon coriander
1/4	teaspoon cloves
1	cup rolled oats
1 1/2	cups oat bran
1	cup black raisins

In a large mixing bowl, whisk together first 4 ingredients until smooth. Mix together flour, baking powder and spices, and add, all at once, whisking just until smooth. Stir in oats, oat bran and raisins. Drop cookie batter by rounded tablespoons on 2 non-stick cookie sheets. Bake in a 350-degree oven for 25 to 30 minutes or until brown. Yields 18 to 20 large cookies.

Spicy Yam Granola Bars

These tasty wholesome bars make great snacks.

1 3/4	cups baked yams, peeled and mashed with a fork (about 1 3/4 pounds)
1/3	cup frozen concentrated orange juice
1/2	teaspoon cloves
1	tablespoon cinnamon
1	teaspoon ginger
4	cups Fruit-Sweetened Oat Bran Granola (see chapter on Basics), or commercial fruit-sweetened brand of granola
1/2	cup black raisins

In a large mixing bowl mix together yams, orange juice and spices. Stir in granola and raisins. Spread this mixture evenly in a 9x13-inch non-stick baking pan, and press it down with hands and finger tips. Bake in a 400-degree oven for 35 minutes, or until set and deep golden brown. When cool, gently loosen sides with a knife, and cut into bars 1 1/2 x 3 inches. Loosen bars gently on bottom with a spatula. Store in refrigerator or freezer. Yields 24 bars.

Crunchy Fruit-Sweetened Mandelbrot
(Almond Cookies)

If you like crunchy snacks, you'll enjoy these. They are made with only the healthiest ingredients. Store Mandelbrot in the refrigerator in an airtight container. Then, crisp them in a 350-degree oven for 3 to 5 minutes, or in a toaster oven for 1 minute.

- 6 egg whites
- 3/4 cup frozen concentrated apple juice
- 1/4 cup frozen concentrated orange juice
- 2 tablespoons oil
- 1 teaspoon vanilla

- 2 1/2 cups whole wheat flour
- 2 teaspoons baking powder
- 2 teaspoons cinnamon

- 1 cup chopped, sliced or slivered almonds (optional)
- 1 cup raisins
- sprinkle of cinnamon for top

Whisk the first 5 ingredients in a mixing bowl. Mix together flour, baking powder and cinnamon, and add, all at once, whisking just until smooth. Then stir in almonds and raisins. For easy shaping of loaves, chill dough overnight or for several hours. Preheat oven to 350 degrees. Shape into 8 small loaves, 4x2x1-inch each. Bake on a non-stick cookie sheet in a 350-degree oven for approximately 30 minutes or until loaves are light brown. Remove loaves from oven.

Cut loaves into slices 1/2-inch thick. Arrange slices on two non-stick cookie sheets. Sprinkle slices with cinnamon and bake for 1 hour in a 225-degree oven or until slices are dry and crispy. Yields approximately 5 dozen Mandelbrot cookies.

Crispy Cereal Snacks

For a special treat some evening, try this crunchy coated cereal.

- 12 cups puffed wheat or puffed rice

- 1/4 cup honey
- 1/2 cup dark molasses
- 1 1/2 teaspoons oil

Place puffed wheat or puffed rice in a large mixing bowl. In a medium-size non-stick saucepan, boil honey, molasses and oil over medium heat until it reaches 260-degrees (hard-ball stage). Remove syrup from the stove, and very carefully and slowly (syrup is very hot) pour it over the puffed cereal, stirring constantly until cereal is evenly coated. Cool before serving. Yields 3 quarts.

Large Wholesome Gingerbread Cookies

These are great for children and grownups alike.

    4   egg whites
    1/2 cup molasses
    1/2 cup honey
    2   tablespoons oil
    2/3 cup non-fat milk

    3 1/2 cups whole wheat flour
    2   teaspoons baking soda
    2   teaspoons ground ginger
    1   tablespoon cinnamon
    1/4 teaspoon cloves

    1   cup black raisins

In a large mixing bowl, whisk together first 5 ingredients until blended. Mix together flour, baking soda, and spices and add, all at once, mixing only until smooth. Do not overbeat. Stir in raisins. On a non-stick cookie sheet, drop cookie batter by heaping tablespoonful to form cookies 3 inches in diameter by 1/2-inch high. Bake in a 400-degree oven for about 12 minutes or until cookies are dry on top. Do not overbake. Yields 16 large cookies.

Chewy Muesli Fruit Cookies

How good it is to reach for marvelous cookies that are good for you, too.

    1   cup banana slices, packed down solidly
    4   egg whites
    1/4 cup frozen concentrated orange juice
    1/2 cup frozen concentrated pineapple juice
    1   tablespoon oil

    1   cup whole wheat flour
    1   teaspoon baking soda

    4   cups Muesli cereal (with raisins and fruit preferred)

In a large mixing bowl, whisk together first 5 ingredients until blended and frothy. Small lumps of banana can remain. Mix together flour and baking soda, and stir it in, mixing only until smooth. With a fork, stir in Muesli cereal just until blended.

Drop cookie batter by heaping teaspoons on a non-stick cookie sheet. Bake cookies in a 375-degree oven for 20 minutes or until light golden brown. Store cookies in refrigerator or freezer. Yields 24 cookies.

Applesauce & Oat Bran Cookies

These cookies are hard to resist. With wholesome ingredients, you can enjoy them to your heart's content.

- 2   egg whites
- 2/3   cup frozen concentrated apple juice
- 1   tablespoon oil
- 2/3   cup Homemade Cinnamon Applesauce (see chapter on Basics), or commercial unsweetened brand, plus 1 teaspoon extra cinnamon

- 1/2   cup whole wheat flour
- 1   cup oat bran
- 1   teaspoon baking soda
- 1   teaspoon nutmeg
- 2   teaspoons cinnamon
- 1/2   teaspoon cloves

- 1/2   cup black raisins
- 1/3   cup chopped walnuts

In a large mixing bowl, whisk together first 4 ingredients until blended. Mix together flour, oat bran, baking soda and spices, and add, all at once, mixing only until smooth. Stir in raisins and nuts. Drop cookie batter by tablespoon onto 2 non-stick cookie sheets, 1-inch apart. Bake cookies in a 400-degree oven for about 15 minutes, or until tops are dry and cookies begin to brown. Remove from cookie sheet with a spatula and store cookies in refrigerator or freezer. Yields 18 large or 24 medium-size cookies.

Fruit-Sweetened Granola Bars

You can enjoy these delicious wholesome bars as snacks, and feel good about eating them.

- 2   cups pureed bananas (about 4 medium-large bananas)
- 5   egg whites
- 1   cup frozen concentrated pineapple juice
- 1/2   cup frozen concentrated orange juice
- 2   tablespoons oil

- 1 1/2   cups whole wheat flour
- 2   teaspoons baking soda
- 1   tablespoon cinnamon
- 1   teaspoon nutmeg

- 8   cups Fruit Sweetened Oat Bran Granola (see chapter on Basics), or commercial fruit sweetened brand of granola
generous sprinkle of cinnamon for top

(Continued)

(Fruit-Sweetened Granola Bars, Cont.)

In a large mixing bowl, whisk together first 5 ingredients until well blended. Mix together flour, baking soda and spices, and add, all at once, whisking only until smooth. Do not overmix. Stir in granola with a fork, only until granola is evenly moistened.

Spread mixture evenly into a 10x15-inch non-stick jelly roll pan with 1/2-inch sides and sprinkle top with cinnamon. Bake in a 400-degree oven for 30 minutes or until top is light golden brown. Cut into 1 1/2x2-inch bars. Store in refrigerator or freezer. Yields 50 bars.

Carrot & Oat Bran Raisin Cookies

These cookies are so innocent and packed with such wholegrain goodness, they can be enjoyed for snacks anytime.

1 1/2   cups oat bran

   1   cup cooked and mashed carrots (about 1/2 pound)
   1   cup frozen concentrated apple juice
   1   tablespoon oil
   1   teaspoon vanilla

   1   cup whole wheat flour
1 1/2   teaspoons baking powder
   1   tablespoon cinnamon
 1/2   teaspoon nutmeg
 1/2   cup black raisins

   4   egg whites, beaten until stiff but not dry

In a 350-degree oven toast oat bran for 15 minutes in a 9x13-inch non-stick baking pan. Meanwhile in a blender or food processor puree carrots with next 3 ingredients until well blended. Pour carrot mixture into a large mixing bowl.

Mix together flour, baking powder, spices, and raisins, and add, all at once, mixing only until smooth. Raise oven temperature to 400-degrees. Fold in oat bran, then beaten egg whites. Drop cookie batter from heaping tablespoons on two non-stick cookie sheets. Bake cookies in a 400-degree oven for approximately 25 minutes or until peaks on cookies are light golden brown. Yields 24 cookies.

Fruit Sweetened Carrot Raisin Chews

These are such favorites that we keep a 5-pound honey can full in the freezer, for a satisfying and healthy snack.

1/2	cup frozen concentrated pineapple juice
1/2	cup frozen concentrated apple juice
4	egg whites
1	teaspoon vanilla
1	cup whole wheat flour
1	teaspoon baking powder
4	teaspoons cinnamon
1	teaspoon nutmeg
1/4	teaspoon cloves
2 1/2	cups rolled oats, uncooked
2	cups grated carrots
3/4	cup black raisins
3/4	cup chopped nuts (optional)

Whisk first 4 ingredients in a large mixing bowl until well blended. Mix together flour, baking powder and spices, and add, all at once, whisking just until blended. Fold in oats, carrots, raisins and nuts. Drop by rounded teaspoons in 2 non-stick cookie sheets, and flatten cookies down with a fork. Bake in a 350-degree oven for approximately 20 minutes, or until brown. Yields 48 cookies.

Munchable Oat Bran Onion Crackers

If you enjoy crunchy onion flavored munchies, you will surely enjoy these. They deliciously contain almost 2 cups of oat bran.

3	egg whites
1/2	tablespoon molasses
2	tablespoons honey
1	tablespoon oil
2	tablespoons caraway seeds
2	tablespoons sesame seeds
1	cup chopped onion, solidly packed down
1/2	cup rye flour or whole wheat flour
1 3/4	cups oat bran
1	teaspoon baking powder
	sprinkle of onion powder for top of crackers

(Continued)

(Oat Bran Onion Crackers, Cont.)

In a large mixing bowl, whisk together first 6 ingredients. Stir in chopped onion. Mix together flour, oat bran and baking powder, and add, all at once, while stirring with a fork just until smooth.

Form dough into small balls the size of walnuts, arrange them on a non-stick cookie sheet, and press balls down into flat crackers, approximately 1 1/2 inches in diameter. Sprinkle tops with onion powder and bake crackers in a 400-degree oven for about 20 minutes or until golden brown on top. Store in air-tight canister. Yields 36 crackers.

Non-Dairy Fruit-Sweetened Carob Brownies

These easy-to-prepare delicious low-fat brownies are so innocent. They are made only with pure wholesome food.

1	cup carob powder
1	cup boiling water

2	teaspoons dark molasses
1	tablespoon vanilla
2	tablespoons oil
8	egg whites
1/2	cup frozen concentrated apple juice
1/3	cup frozen concentrated pineapple juice
2/3	cup water

1 3/4	cups whole wheat flour
2	teaspoons baking powder

1/2	cup broken walnuts (optional)

In a large mixing bowl dissolve carob powder in boiling water. Stir in the next 7 ingredients, and beat with a whisk until well blended. Mix together flour and baking powder, and add, all at once, mixing with a whisk, just until smooth. Do not overmix. Fold in walnuts. Spread batter evenly in a 10x15-inch non-stick jelly roll pan with 1/2-inch sides. Bake brownies in a 375-degree oven for 45 minutes or until brownies test done. Do not overbake. Brownies should be moist. Cut into 2 x 3-inch bars or smaller if desired. Yields 25 brownies.

Carob, Carrot, Oat Bran Cereal Chews

This combination of carob, carrots and oat bran cereal makes these cookies a tasty, wholesome treat.

4	egg whites
1/2	cup frozen concentrated orange juice
1/2	cup frozen concentrated pineapple juice
1	tablespoon oil
1	teaspoon vanilla
1	teaspoon dark molasses
1/2	cup non-fat or low-fat yogurt
1	cup whole wheat flour
1 1/2	teaspoons baking soda
1/2	cup carob powder
1	tablespoon cinnamon
1 1/2	cups grated carrots
3	cups oat bran cereal flakes
1/2	cup black raisins
1/2	cup walnut chunks (optional)

Whisk first 7 ingredients in a large mixing bowl until well blended. Mix together flour, baking soda, carob powder and cinnamon, and add, all at once, whisking just until blended. Gently stir in last 4 ingredients with a fork. Drop by rounded tablespoons, into large mounds, on 2 non-stick cookie sheets. Do not flatten cookies down. Bake cookies in a 375-degree oven for about 20 minutes, or until top and bottom are dry and center is moist. Store in refrigerator or freezer. Yields 20 large cookies.

Brown Rice, Poppy & Sesame Seed Cookies

These firm, nutritious cookies make perfect snacks.

4	egg whites
1/2	cup frozen concentrated orange juice
1/2	cup frozen concentrated pineapple juice
2	tablespoons honey
1/2	cup water
1	teaspoon vanilla
1	tablespoon cinnamon
1/4	teaspoon cloves
1/4	teaspoon coriander
1/4	teaspoon ginger
1/4	teaspoon nutmeg
1	tablespoon oil
1 1/2	cups whole wheat flour
2	teaspoons baking powder

(Continued)

(Brown Rice, Poppy & Sesame Seed Cookies, Cont.)

        6   cups cooked brown rice
        1   cup raisins
       1/3 cup poppy seeds (optional)
       1/4 cup sesame seeds (optional)
            sprinkle of cinnamon for top

In a large mixing bowl, whisk together first 12 ingredients until well blended. Mix together flour and baking powder, and add, all at once, mixing just until smooth. Stir in brown rice, raisins, and seeds. Drop batter by heaping tablespoons on two non-stick cookie sheets. Flatten tops with spoon, and sprinkle them generously with cinnamon. Bake cookies in a 450-degree oven for 25 minutes, or until firm and brown on top and bottom. Store them in refrigerator or freezer until ready to use. Yields 48 cookies.

Carob Oat Bran Cookies

These low-fat cookies are full of fiber and fruit. They taste great frozen too.

       1/2 cup water
       1/2 cup black raisins
        15 pitted dates

       1/2 cup carob powder

        2   tablespoons orange marmalade, fruit sweetened
       1/3 cup non-fat or low-fat yogurt
        3   egg whites
        1   teaspoon vanilla
        1   tablespoon oil
      1 1/2 teaspoons dark molasses

       1/2 cup whole wheat flour
        1   teaspoon baking soda

        2   cups oat bran flakes

In a small non-stick saucepan bring the water, raisins and dates to a boil, and cook for 1 minute. Remove pan from heat, and stir in carob powder. Blend this mixture, along with the next 6 ingredients in a food processor or blender. Then place this mixture into a large mixing bowl. Mix together the flour and baking soda, and add, all at once, stirring only until smooth. Fold in oat bran flakes. Drop cookie batter by rounded tablespoon, and bake cookies in a non-stick cookie sheet at 400-degrees for 12 to 15 minutes. Yields 18 cookies.

Chapter 7

Mouth-Watering Pastries, Coffee Cakes and Oven-Baked Pancakes

Now you can treat yourself and your loved ones to delicious mouth-watering wholegrain pastries and coffee cakes that will please your sweet-tooth and provide your body with the nutrients it needs. In contrast, most sweet rolls and coffee cakes have only empty calories and sugar that depletes your own body resources.

In this section you will also find recipes for delicious and wholesome oven-baked pancakes. Imagine the pleasure of being able to prepare light, low-fat, low-cholesterol wholegrain pancakes in minutes, smothered with innocent fruit sweetened syrups.

Most pancakes are made with white flour, whole eggs, butter or margarine, whole milk and sugar. Our pancake recipes call for wholegrain flour, fruit juices, egg whites, buttermilk, non-fat yogurt, 1 teaspoon oil, and spices. What a fun, healthy way to start out the day!

Whole Wheat Cinnamon Buns

The aroma of these cinnamon buns baking is divine, as is the treat of eating such a delicious wholesome treat.

    1   recipe Sweet Yeast Pastry Dough (see chapter on Basics)

    1   cup raisins
    1   tablespoon cinnamon
    1/2 cup frozen concentrated apple juice

    1/3 cup honey
         generous sprinkle of cinnamon for top

While dough is rising, mix together raisins, cinnamon, and apple juice in a small non-stick saucepan. Bring mixture to a boil, then reduce heat, and simmer for 5 minutes. Remove from heat, stir in honey and set aside.

On a floured board roll out prepared dough into a rectangle 10x14 inches. Spread raisin-cinnamon syrup mixture over dough, roll up dough into a long roll, and cut roll into 8 slices, each 1 3/4 inches thick. Arrange cinnamon buns cut side down in a 9-inch round non-stick baking pan. Let dough rise until doubled in bulk. Bake buns in a 375-degree oven for 20 minutes or until deep golden brown. Do not overbake. Yields 8 large cinnamon buns.

Whole Wheat Sticky Buns

These sticky buns are sure to bring raves. They happen to be our son, Dan's, favorite and he has very good taste.

Dough:
   1/2   recipe Whole Wheat Pastry Dough (see chapter on Basics)

Filling:
  1 1/2   cups raisins
    1   cup frozen concentrated frozen apple juice

    1   cup chopped pecans (optional)
    4   teaspoons cinnamon
   1/2   cup honey

Honey Syrup:
  1 1/2   cups honey
   2/3   cup water

   24   pecan halves or pitted date halves to decorate top of buns

Prepare Whole Wheat Pastry Dough as instructed in recipe. While dough is rising prepare filling and syrup.

To prepare filling: In a medium-size saucepan bring raisins and apple juice to a boil, and cook raisins for 15 minutes. Remove from heat. In a medium-size mixing bowl combine the next 3 ingredients, add plumped raisins, with the juice, and mix well.

To prepare syrup: In a medium-size saucepan bring the honey and water to a boil and cook syrup over low heat for 3 minutes, watching that syrup does not boil over.

To assemble: Spread 1 1/2 tablespoons of syrup into 24 muffin cups, and place 1/2 pecan or 1/2 date into the center of each cup. Cut dough into 2 parts, and roll each piece into a 6x18-inch rectangle on a floured board. Gently spread half of the filling on top of each rectangle, and roll up each rectangle into a long roll. Cut each roll into twelve 1 1/2-inch pieces. Press each piece, cut-side down, into each muffin cup and let dough rise again, in a warm place, until double in bulk. Bake buns in a 375-degree oven for 20 to 25 minutes or until buns are golden brown. Cool buns for 20 minutes, then remove them from pan. Yields 24 buns.

Honey Cinnamon Raisin Pastry Ring

If you love cinnamon, you'll adore this sweet pastry ring.

    1/2   recipe Sweet Cinnamon Pastry Dough (see chapter on Basics)

    1/2   cup honey
      1   tablespoon oil
    1/2   cup black raisins
    1/2   cup chopped walnuts (optional)
          grated zest of 1/2 large orange, (orange part of the peel)

      1   egg white
      1   tablespoon honey
    1/2   teaspoon cinnamon

Prepare Sweet Cinnamon Pastry Dough. While dough is rising, in a medium-size mixing bowl, mix together honey, oil, raisins, and walnuts.

After the first rising punch dough down, place dough on lightly floured board, and flatten dough into an 8x12-inch rectangle with hands.

Spread honey-raisin mixture evenly on top of dough and roll dough lengthwise into a roll. Join ends of roll together forming a circle. Make cuts 1 inch apart in outer edge, leaving center circle intact. Gently lift ring into a 9-inch round non-stick baking pan, and lay slices down forming a pattern. Mix together egg white, honey and cinnamon with a fork. Brush top of ring generously with glaze, and keep it in a warm place to rise again. Bake pastry ring in a 375-degree oven for 20 to 25 minutes, or until light golden brown on top. Serve warm. Serves 8.

Poppy Seed Pastry Ring

This lovely pastry ring is both delicious and nutritious.

    1/2   recipe Sweet Cinnamon Pastry Dough (see chapter on Basics)

Poppy Seed Filling:
    1/2   cup poppy seeds
    1/2   cup non-fat milk
    1/4   cup honey
      2   teaspoons cinnamon

    1/2   cup black raisins

  1 1/2   teaspoons honey
  1 1/2   teaspoons water

(Continued)

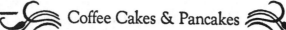

(Poppy Seed Pastry Ring, Cont.)

Follow instructions for Sweet Cinnamon Pastry Dough. While dough is rising prepare Poppy Seed Filling. In a medium size non-stick saucepan mix together first 4 ingredients. Cook over medium heat, stirring frequently, until mixture thickens. Stir in raisins, cook 1 minute longer, and remove filling from stove. Filling should be moist.

After pastry dough has doubled in bulk, roll or press out 1/2 recipe of the dough on a lightly floured board into a rectangle 8x12 inches. Spread cooled poppy seed filling evenly on top of dough, and roll it up lengthwise. Join ends of roll together into a circle, and cut 1-inch slices almost through circle, leaving center of circle intact. Gently lift pastry ring into a 9-inch round non-stick baking pan. Turn slices on their side, forming a design. Mix together honey and water, brush mixture on top of pastry ring, and keep pastry in a warm place until double in bulk. Bake in a 375-degree oven for 20 to 25 minutes or until light golden brown. Serve warm. Serves 8.

Light Oat Bran Cereal Streusel Coffee Cake

This is a great way to enjoy your oat bran.

- 2 cups oat bran flakes
- 1/4 cup frozen concentrated orange juice
- 2 teaspoons cinnamon

- 6 egg whites
- 2/3 cup buttermilk
- 1/2 cup frozen concentrated orange juice
- 1 tablespoon oil
- 2 tablespoons honey

- 1 cup whole wheat pastry flour
- 2 teaspoons baking soda
- 2 teaspoons cinnamon
- 1/2 cup black raisins

Coarsely chop the first 3 ingredients in a blender or food processor. Reserve 1/3 of this mixture for topping, and spread the remainder evenly in a 9x9-inch non-stick baking pan.

In a large mixing bowl, whisk together egg whites, buttermilk, orange juice, oil, and honey until blended. Mix together flour, baking soda, cinnamon and raisins, and add, all at once, mixing just until smooth. Pour batter in cereal-lined baking pan, and sprinkle reserved crushed cereal mixture on top. Bake coffee cake in a 350-degree oven for 40 to 45 minutes or until cake tests done. Serves 6 to 8.

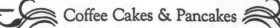 
Breakfast Coffee Cake

Oh what a beautiful morning...especially when you bite into this delicious rich-tasting coffee cake. It is innocent, made with egg whites, whole wheat pastry flour, low-fat yogurt, fruit juice, honey, and so little oil. You'll want to bake this one over and over again.

1/4	cup frozen concentrated orange juice
1/4	cup honey
2	tablespoons oil
4	egg whites
1/2	cup low-fat yogurt
1	teaspoon vanilla
1 1/3	cups whole wheat pastry flour
1/2	teaspoon baking soda
1	teaspoon baking powder
1	teaspoon cinnamon
1/3	cup chopped walnuts
1/2	cup black raisins
1	tablespoon cinnamon
1	tablespoon carob powder
1	tablespoon honey for top

In a large mixing bowl, whisk together first 6 ingredients until blended. Mix together flour, baking soda, baking powder and cinnamon, and add, all at once, mixing only until smooth. Do not overmix. In a small bowl mix together nuts, raisins, cinnamon and carob powder.

To assemble: Spread 1/2 of the batter in a 9-inch round non-stick baking pan. Sprinkle 1/2 of raisin-nut mixture on top. Repeat, spreading the remainder of the batter, then the raisin-nut mixture on top. Slowly drizzle 1 tablespoon of honey over the top. Bake in a 350-degree oven for 30 minutes or until coffee cake is golden brown on top and tests done. Serves 6.

Orange Pastry Buns

If you like orange flavored sweet rolls try these.

1/2	recipe Sweet Cinnamon Pastry Dough (see chapter on Basics)

Orange Filling:
3/4	cup frozen concentrated orange juice
3/4	cup cold water
2	tablespoons lemon juice
1/4	cup honey
3	tablespoons cornstarch or potato starch
2	tablespoons cold water

(Continued)

(Orange Pastry Buns, Cont.)

Prepare Sweet Cinnamon Pastry Dough as per instructions. While dough is rising prepare Orange Filling. In a medium-size non-stick saucepan, heat together orange juice, water, lemon juice and honey. Bring mixture to a boil and then, over medium heat, cook for 5 minutes. Mix together the cornstarch or potato starch and water, add this mixture, and stir constantly while filling thickens. Remove from heat and cool.

When dough has doubled in bulk, roll or press dough into a rectangular sheet 1/4 to 1/2 inches thick. Spread 2/3 of the orange filling evenly on top of dough and gently roll dough up lengthwise into a roll. Cut roll into 12 slices, arrange slices cut side down in a 9-inch round non-stick baking pan. Spread remaining 1/3 of the orange filling evenly on top of buns, and keep them in a warm place until double in bulk. Bake in a 375-degree oven for 20 to 25 minutes or until golden brown. Serve warm. Pull buns apart with a fork. Serves 8.

Pastry Buns With Cheese Raisin Filling

These low-cholesterol cheese filled pastry buns are rich tasting and simply scrumptious.

- 1   **recipe Sweet Yeast Pastry Dough (see chapter on Basics)**

- 1 1/2   **cups low-fat cottage cheese**
- 3   **tablespoons cornstarch or potato starch**
- 3   **tablespoons honey**

- 1   **cup black raisins**

- 1/4   **cup chopped pecans (optional)**

Follow instructions for preparing Sweet Pastry Dough. After dough has risen double its bulk, punch the soft dough down and place the dough wrapped in plastic wrap in the freezer for 45 minutes, or until firm enough to work with. Meanwhile prepare cheese filling.

In a blender or food processor blend the cottage cheese, cornstarch or potato starch and honey until smooth and creamy. Pour mixture into a medium size mixing bowl, stir in raisins and set aside.

To assemble pastry buns, remove the dough from freezer. Cut dough into 12 equal parts. Place one part into each of 12 muffin cups and with moistened fingers, press dough on the bottom and up the sides of each muffin cup. Spoon cheese filling evenly into each muffin cup and sprinkle top with chopped pecans. Place pan in a warm place until dough doubles in bulk. Bake in a 350-degree oven for 20 minutes. Do not overbake. Yields 12.

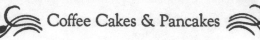 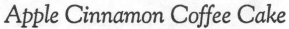

Apple Cinnamon Coffee Cake

For a delicious nutritious coffee cake full of apples and cinnamon, bake this one, then enjoy it without guilt.

Batter:
- 1/4 cup frozen concentrated apple juice
- 1/4 cup honey
- 2 tablespoons oil
- 4 egg whites
- 1/2 cup low-fat yogurt
- 1 teaspoon vanilla

- 1 1/3 cups whole wheat pastry flour
- 1/2 teaspoon baking soda
- 1 teaspoon baking powder
- 2 teaspoons cinnamon
- 1/2 teaspoon nutmeg

Filling:
- 2 cups coarsely chopped apples (1 large red or golden delicious apple, unpeeled)
- 1 tablespoon cinnamon
- 1/2 cup black raisins
- sprinkle of cinnamon for top

In a large mixing bowl, whisk together first 6 ingredients until blended. Mix together the flour, baking soda, baking powder, and spices, and add, all at once, mixing only until smooth. Do not overmix. In a small bowl mix together the chopped apple, cinnamon and raisins.

To assemble: Spread 1/2 the batter in a 9-inch round non-stick baking pan. Sprinkle the chopped apple mixture evenly over batter, then spread the remainder of the batter evenly on top of the chopped apples. Sprinkle top generously with cinnamon, and bake in a 350-degree oven for 30 to 35 minutes, or until coffee cake is golden brown on top and tests done. Serves 6.

Baked Orange Buttermilk Pancakes

This light, delicious fruit sweetened wholegrain pancake is a great healthy way to start the day.

- 1/4 cup frozen concentrated orange juice
- 1 cup buttermilk
- 3 egg whites
- 1 teaspoon oil

- 2/3 cup whole wheat flour
- 1 1/2 teaspoons baking soda

(Continued)

(Baked Orange Buttermilk Pancakes, Cont.)

    1   teaspoon oil for pans

2 to 4   tablespoons frozen concentrated orange juice, thawed, for topping
    2   slices of orange for garnish (optional)

Heat two 9-inch round non-stick baking pans in a preheated 450-degree oven for 10 minutes. In a medium-size mixing bowl whisk together first 4 ingredients until blended. Mix together flour and baking soda, and add, all at once, mixing just until smooth. Do not overmix. Spread 1/2 teaspoon oil around bottom of each pan with a piece of paper towel. Divide batter between the pans.

Bake pancakes in a preheated 450-degree oven for 10 to 12 minutes, or until pancakes are brown and begin to pull away from the sides of the pan. Serve immediately with concentrated orange juice for topping. Garnish with a slice of fresh orange. Serves 2 to 3.

Oven-Baked Walnut Oat Bran Pancakes

These unusual pancakes make a well-balanced, wholesome breakfast treat.

    4   egg whites
    3/4   cup buttermilk
    1/3   cup frozen concentrated orange juice
    1   teaspoon cinnamon
    1/2   teaspoon vanilla
    1   teaspoon oil
    2   tablespoons honey

    1/2   cup whole wheat flour
1 1/2   teaspoons baking soda
    3/4   cup oat bran

    2   tablespoons poppy seeds
    1/4   cup chopped walnuts (optional)
    2   tablespoons raw wheat germ (optional)

    1   teaspoon oil for pans

Preheat oven to 450-degrees. Heat two 9-inch round, ungreased, non-stick baking pans. In a medium-size mixing bowl whisk together first 7 ingredients. Mix together flour, baking soda and oat bran, and add, all at once, mixing just until smooth. Stir in poppy seeds, walnuts and wheat germ. Carefully remove heated baking pans, rub with oil, and spread 1/2 of pancake batter in each pan. Bake pancakes in a 450-degree oven for 8 minutes, and serve immediately with pure maple syrup or your favorite fruit-sweetened jam. Serves 2 to 4.

Easy, Oven-Baked, Apple Oat Bran Pancakes

You're sure to find this a delicious, wholesome breakfast.

        3   egg whites
      1/4   cup frozen concentrated apple juice
      1/4   cup plain non-fat or low-fat yogurt
      1/2   cup non-fat milk
        1   teaspoon oil
        2   teaspoons cinnamon
      1/2   teaspoon nutmeg

      1/2   cup oat bran
      1/3   cup whole wheat flour
        1   teaspoon baking powder

      2/3   cup chopped sweet apples

      1/2   teaspoon oil for pan

Preheat an ungreased 9-inch round non-stick cake pan in a 450-degree oven for 5 minutes. In a medium-size mixing bowl whisk together the first 7 ingredients until blended. Mix together oat bran, flour and baking powder, and add, all at once, mixing only until smooth. Fold in chopped apples.

Remove heated cake pan carefully from the oven. With a paper towel, brush bottom with oil and immediately pour pancake batter into the pan. Bake pancake in a 450-degree oven for 12 minutes. Enjoy this pancake with your favorite syrup or jam. Serves 2.

Easy, Oven-Baked, Banana Oat Bran Pancake:
Follow recipe for Easy Oven Baked Apple Pancakes making the following substitutions: Omit chopped apples and substitute 1/2 cup of chopped bananas; and omit nutmeg and substitute 1/2 teaspoon coriander.

Baked Pineapple Almond Pancakes

These wholesome fruit sweetened pancakes are an exciting beginning to a healthy, low-fat day.

        4   egg whites
      1/3   cup frozen concentrated pineapple juice
    1 1/2   cups buttermilk
        1   teaspoon oil
        1   teaspoon vanilla
            grated zest of 1 small lemon (yellow part of the peel)

        1   cup whole wheat flour
        2   teaspoons baking soda
        2   teaspoons cinnamon

(Continued)

(Baked Pineapple Almond Pancakes, Cont.)

1/3   cup slivered almonds (optional)

1   teaspoon oil for pans

1/4   cup frozen concentrated pineapple juice, thawed, for topping

In a large mixing bowl, whisk together first 6 ingredients until blended. Mix together the flour, baking soda and cinnamon, and add, all at once, mixing until smooth. Do not overbeat. Fold in almonds.

Meanwhile heat two 9-inch round non-stick baking pans in a preheated 450-degree oven for 10 minutes. Remove pans from oven and with a paper towel, spread 1/2 teaspoon oil on bottom of each pan. Divide batter between the pans.

Bake pancakes in 450-degree oven for 10 minutes, or until pancakes are brown and begin to pull away from the sides of the pan. During last 5 minutes of baking spread the concentrated pineapple juice on top. Serves 2 to 4.

Baked Banana Yogurt Pancakes

These wholesome fruit-sweetened pancakes make a delicious breakfast or brunch treat.

1/3   cup frozen concentrated apple juice
1/2   cup non-fat or low-fat yogurt
1   cup non-fat milk
4   egg whites
1   teaspoon oil
1   teaspoon lemon juice
1   teaspoon vanilla

1   cup whole wheat flour
2   teaspoons baking soda
1   teaspoon cinnamon

1   large ripe banana, thinly sliced

1   teaspoon oil for cake pans

Preheat oven to 450-degrees, and heat 2 ungreased, round 9-inch non-stick baking pans. In a large mixing bowl whisk together first 7 ingredients until blended. Mix flour, baking soda and cinnamon, and add, all at once, mixing with a whisk only until smooth. Do not overmix. Fold in sliced bananas.

Remove cake pans from oven, and grease each pan with 1/2 teaspoon oil. Spread 1/2 of batter in each pan and bake pancakes in a 450-degree oven for 12 minutes, or until they are brown and begin to pull away from sides of pan. Serve immediately with maple syrup or fruit-sweetened jam. Serves 2 to 4.

Baked Buttermilk Pancakes With Syrupy Apple Slices

These light delicious wholegrain pancakes with syrupy apple slices make a great brunch item for 2 to 4 people.

2	large delicious apples
2/3	cup concentrated apple juice
2	teaspoons cinnamon

1/3	cup frozen concentrated apple juice
1 1/2	cups buttermilk
4	egg whites
1	teaspoon oil
1	teaspoon vanilla

1	cup whole wheat flour
2	teaspoons baking soda
1	tablespoon cinnamon
1	teaspoon oil for 2 pans

In a medium-size non-stick saucepan, cook first 3 ingredients, uncovered, over medium heat, stirring occasionally until mixture comes to a boil. Reduce heat to low, cover pan, and let slices steam while baking pancakes.

Meanwhile prepare pancake batter: In a large mixing bowl whisk together next 5 ingredients until blended. Mix together flour, baking soda and cinnamon, and add, all at once, whisking only until smooth. Do not overmix.

Heat two 9-inch round non-stick baking pans in a preheated 450-degree oven for 10 minutes. Remove pans from oven and, with a paper towel, spread 1/2 teaspoon of oil on bottom of each pan. Divide batter between the pans. Bake in a 450-degree oven for 10 minutes, or until pancakes are brown and begin to pull away from the sides of pan. Serve immediately with syrupy apple slices on top. Serves 2 to 4.

Fluffy Apple Pancake Treat

For a special treat, try this light, low-fat, delicious and nutritious pancake.

1	red or golden delicious apple, peeled and cut into 16 to 20 thin wedges
1 1/2	teaspoons cinnamon
1	tablespoon honey

6	egg whites
2	tablespoons frozen concentrated apple juice
1/2	cup non-fat or low-fat yogurt
1	teaspoon oil

1/2	cup whole wheat pastry flour
1/2	teaspoon baking soda
2	teaspoons cinnamon
1/4	teaspoon nutmeg
1	teaspoon oil for pan
	sprinkle of nutmeg on top

(Continued)

(Fluffy Apple Pancake, Cont.)

Toss apple wedges, cinnamon, and honey in a small bowl, and set aside. In a medium-size mixing bowl whisk together next 4 ingredients until blended. Mix together flour, baking soda and spices, and add, all at once mixing only until smooth.

Heat a 9-inch round non-stick baking pan in a preheated 450-degree oven for 10 minutes. Remove pan from oven and spread oil in pan. Using a spoon quickly arrange apple slices evenly on bottom. Pour pancake batter on top of apple slices. Sprinkle top with nutmeg. Bake in a 450-degree oven for 10 to 12 minutes or until pancake begins to pull away from the sides of the pan. Remove from oven. Gently loosen sides and bottom with a spatula, and flip pancake onto a large platter. Serve at once. Serves 2.

Jam Filled Pastry Strips

What could satisfy a sweet tooth more innocently than these pastry strips made with bananas and fruit-sweetened jam?

1/4	cup warm water (105 degrees)
2	envelopes active dry yeast
1 1/4	cups pureed bananas (3 small ripe bananas)
2	tablespoons lemon juice
	grated zest of 1 lemon, (yellow part of the peel)
3	tablespoons oil
1/2	teaspoon coriander
1/2	teaspoon cardamom
2	cups whole wheat pastry flour
1	10-ounce jar blueberry jam, fruit sweetened
1/2	cup slivered almonds (optional)
1	egg white
1	tablespoon honey

In a large bowl of an electric mixer dissolve yeast granules in warm water. Beat in next 6 ingredients until smooth, then add flour and beat on medium speed for 5 minutes. Cover and keep dough in a warm place until double in bulk. Punch dough down and chill or freeze until firm enough to handle. Divide dough in half and work quickly before dough softens. Press each half of dough into a rectangle 12x4 inches between 2 pieces of plastic wrap. Spread 1/2 of jam over each rectangle and 1/2 of the almonds over the jam, reserving 1/2 of almonds for top.

Using plastic wrap to help lift the dough, fold rectangles in half lengthwise and arrange them in a non-stick cookie or jelly roll pan several inches apart. Mix together honey and egg white, brush tops of pastry rolls and sprinkle almonds on top. Keep dough in a warm place until double in bulk, and bake pastries in a 350-degree oven for 20 to 25 minutes or until light golden brown. Do not overbake. Yields 2 large pastry strips.

Chapter 8

Passover Specialties

Passover baked goods are traditionally made with whole eggs, a lot of oil, and white sugar. We use egg whites, fresh fruit juice, yams, bananas, dates, raisins, honey, potato starch, cake meal or whole wheat matzo finely ground in the blender, and very little oil.

After a big holiday meal your family and guests will especially enjoy the wholesome sponge cakes and baked Passover delicacies found in this section. Please be aware that sponge cakes made with honey do not rise as high and are not as light and fluffy as those made with sugar. If ground whole wheat matzo is used in place of cake meal, you can expect the sponge cake to be even less light, but still wholesome and delicious. You and your loved ones can help keep your arteries more free from cholesterol and plaque build-up and still enjoy this festive occasion.

Large Passover Fruit Scones

These easy-to-prepare wholesome fruit scones are excellent for breakfast, snacks and high tea.

1	cup finely chopped apples, packed down solidly
1	cup chopped walnuts
1/4	cup grape juice or orange juice
2	teaspoons cinnamon
1	tablespoon oil
1/4	cup honey
8	egg whites
1	teaspoon cider vinegar
1/2	cup potato starch
1/2	cup Passover cake meal (or 1/2 cup finely ground whole wheat matzo)
2	teaspoons baking soda
1 1/2	cups black raisins

In a medium-size mixing bowl mix together the first 6 ingredients. In the large bowl of an electric mixer, beat together the egg whites with vinegar until whites are stiff, but not dry. Gently fold the apple-nut mixture into the beaten whites. Mix together the potato starch, cake meal and baking soda, and gently fold in these dry ingredients just until blended; then fold in raisins. Drop batter by heaping tablespoons on a non-stick or lightly oiled 10x15-inch baking sheet. Bake in a 400-degree oven for 25 minutes, or until deep golden brown. Yields 14 large scones.

Passover Vanilla Pudding

This delicious low-fat vanilla pudding is perfect for the Passover trifle, and can be enjoyed on its own.

1	cup non-fat milk
1/2	cup honey
1/2	cup dry non-fat milk powder
1 3/4	cups non-fat milk
4	tablespoons potato starch
1/4	cup water
2	teaspoons vanilla

In the bottom of a double boiler, bring 3-inches of water to a boil. Meanwhile, blend the first 3 ingredients in a blender or food processor until smooth. Pour this mixture into the top of double boiler, and stir in remaining non-fat milk. Cook over medium heat stirring occasionally for 20 minutes.

Mix together potato starch with water until smooth and quickly stir it into the milk mixture, to avoid lumps. Continue cooking pudding over low heat for 10 minutes longer, stirring occasionally. Remove from heat, stir in vanilla, and chill. Yields 3 1/2 cups.

Passover Trifle

This elegant dessert can be prepared the night before or in the morning of the day you plan to serve it. Your guests' raves will make it well worth the effort.

1/2	Passover Orange Sponge Cake (see Index)
	double recipe Passover Vanilla Pudding (see Index)
1/3	cup fresh orange juice or grape juice
1/2	cup berry jam, fruit sweetened
3	boxes fresh strawberries

Cut sponge cake into slices 1/2-inch thick, and set aside. Prepare a double recipe of the pudding and chill well. Have juice ready, and set it aside. Wash, hull, drain and slice strawberries in thirds lengthwise.

Layer 1/2 of the sponge cake slices in the bottom of a decorative 3-quart glass bowl. Pour 1/2 of the juice on top of cake slices, spread 1/2 of jam on top of cake layer, then 1/2 of the pudding over cake slices, and arrange 1/2 of the sliced berries on top. Repeat all these layers, ending with sliced strawberries on top. Chill well before serving. Serves 12.

Passover Cheesecake

This delicious cheesecake is a delight to serve all year long. Serve with fresh sliced strawberries over each portion, or decorate on top of cake.

Lemon Honey Nut Crust:

1/2	cup Passover cake meal (or 1/2 cup finely ground whole wheat matzo, ground in blender)
	grated zest of 1 large lemon (yellow part of the peel)
1/2	cup chopped walnuts or pecans
1	egg white
1	teaspoon lemon juice
1	tablespoon honey
1	tablespoon oil
1/2	teaspoon vanilla
1	teaspoon water
1	tablespoon honey

In a medium-size bowl mix together the cake meal, lemon zest and nuts. In a small bowl beat the next 6 ingredients, and stir this into dry ingredients with a fork until moisture is absorbed. Form dough with hands, and press dough into a thin crust in the bottom of a 9x9-inch glass oven-proof baking pan. With finger tips bring crust 1/4 to 1/2 inch up the sides. Brush or rub 1 tablespoon of honey on top of crust for a glaze, then bake crust in a 400-degree oven for 10 minutes. Remove from oven and set aside.

Cheesecake Filling:

4	cups low-fat cottage cheese
3/4	cup honey
5	tablespoons potato starch
3	tablespoons dry non-fat milk powder
	rind of 2 lemons
	rind of 2 oranges
6	egg whites
1/2	teaspoon vanilla

Reduce oven temperature to 350-degrees. Blend cottage cheese in a blender or food processor until very smooth and place in a large mixing bowl. Blend next 7 ingredients, and stir mixture into whipped cottage cheese until thoroughly mixed. Pour batter into prepared Lemon Honey Nut Crust. Bake in a 350-degree oven for 25 to 30 minutes or until puffed slightly. Do not overbake. Filling will thicken as it cools. Cool cake and then chill for several hours before serving. Serves 8 to 10.

Passover Lemon Meringue Party Cake

This beautiful, delicious, light dessert is the perfect end of a holiday meal. The sponge cake can be made ahead of time and frozen.

1	Passover Lemon Sponge Cake (see Index)
	grated zest of 2 large lemons (yellow part of the peel)
1/2	cup fresh lemon juice
2 1/4	cups fresh orange juice
2	tablespoons oil
2/3	cup honey
1/2	cup potato starch
6	egg whites
8	egg whites
1	teaspoon cider vinegar
1/3	cup honey

Line the bottom of a 9x13-inch baking pan with 3/4-inch thick slices of sponge cake. To form a solid cake layer, fill in the gaps with small pieces.

In a small bowl mix together the grated lemon zest and lemon juice, and set aside. In a large non-stick pan mix together the next 4 ingredients and set aside. In a large bowl of an electric mixer beat 6 egg whites until stiff but not dry, and set aside.

Heat ingredients in pan over medium heat, stirring constantly just until mixture thickens. Immediately stir in beaten egg whites for 1 minute longer, then remove from heat. Stir in lemon juice and rind until smooth. Spread lemon pudding evenly over cake layer.

Preheat oven to 400-degrees. In a large bowl of an electric mixer beat 8 egg whites with vinegar until foamy. Add honey and continue beating on high speed until whites are stiff and glossy. Spread meringue evenly on lemon pudding layer. To decorate top make several wide lazy S's across top of meringue. Bake meringue cake in a 400-degree oven for 7 to 9 minutes, or until meringue peaks are deep golden brown. Chill well before serving. Serves 12 to 16.

Passover Spice Sponge Cake

This light delicately flavored sponge cake can be enjoyed to your heart's content.

- 3/4   cup honey

- 1/4   cup fresh lemon juice
- 4   egg whites
     grated zest of 1 large lemon (yellow part of the peel)
     grated zest of 1 large orange (orange part of the peel)
- 1/2   cup chopped walnuts
- 2   tablespoons oil
- 1   teaspoon vanilla

- 1/2   cup Passover cake meal (or 1/2 cup finely ground whole wheat matzo)
- 1/2   cup potato starch
- 1   tablespoon cinnamon
- 1/2   teaspoon ginger

- 8   egg whites

In a medium-size non-stick saucepan bring the honey to a boil, and cook it over low heat for 5 minutes. Use caution as honey can overflow if heat is too high.

Meanwhile in a large mixing bowl, beat the next 7 ingredients until smooth. Mix together cake meal, potato starch, and spices, and add all at once, mixing just until smooth.

In a large bowl of an electric mixer beat egg whites until foamy, then while beating on highest speed, add hot honey in a thin, steady stream. Continue beating whites only until they hold soft peaks. Do not overbeat or the cake will be too dry. Fold in whites 1/3 at a time to the cake batter just until whites disappear. Spread batter into an ungreased 10-inch tube cake pan. Gently circle through the batter a few times with a knife to release air bubbles.

Bake cake in a 350-degree oven for approximately 30 minutes or until top is very light golden brown and cake tests done. Invert cake pan immediately until cake is cool. This cake can be made ahead of time and frozen, then thawed before serving. Serves 10 to 12.

Passover Honey Cake

This moist, delicious honey cake is a real treat.

grated zest of 3 medium oranges (orange part of the peel)
grated zest of 2 large lemons (yellow part of the peel)

4	egg whites
1	cup honey
1	cup fresh orange juice
1	tablespoon oil
2	teaspoons vanilla

1 1/2	cups Passover cake meal (or 1 1/2 cups finely ground whole wheat matzo)
1	tablespoon baking soda
1	tablespoon cinnamon

3/4	cup black raisins
3/4	cup chopped walnuts
4	egg whites

Place zests in a mixing bowl. Stir in next 5 ingredients until blended. Mix together cake meal, baking soda and cinnamon and add, all at once, mixing just until smooth. Stir in raisins and walnuts. In the small bowl of an electric mixer beat the 4 egg whites until stiff but not dry. Gently fold beaten egg whites into the cake batter. Spread batter in a lightly oiled 10-inch tube baking pan, and bake in a 350-degree oven for 45 minutes, or until cake tests done. Do not invert cake pan. Serves 12.

Passover Orange Sponge Cake

This is a great tasting sponge cake. We use this one to make a triffle. It can be made ahead and frozen.

1	cup honey
	grated zest of 3 large oranges (orange part of the peel)
	grated zest of 2 large lemons (yellow part of the peel)
1	tablespoon fresh lemon juice

1/2	cup fresh orange juice
4	egg whites
1	teaspoon vanilla

2/3	cup potato starch
2/3	cup Passover cake meal (or 2/3 cup finely ground whole wheat matzo)
10	egg whites

(Continued)

(Passover Orange Sponge Cake, Cont.)

In a medium-size non-stick pan, bring the honey to a boil and cook it, over low heat, for 5 minutes. Use caution as honey can overflow, if heat is too high. Place zests, lemon juice and the next 3 ingredients in a mixing bowl and beat until thoroughly mixed. Mix together potato starch and cake meal and fold these dry ingredients in, just until blended.

In a large bowl of an electric mixer beat the egg whites until foamy. Then, while beating at high speed, gradually add honey in a fine stream. Continue beating just until whites are stiff enough to hold soft peaks. Do not overbeat or cake will be too dry. Gently fold in egg whites 1/3 at a time to the cake batter just until whites disappear. Do not overmix. Spread batter evenly in an ungreased 10-inch tube pan, and circle around through the batter several times with a knife to release air bubbles. Bake cake in a 350-degree oven for approximately 35 minutes or until cake tests done. Do not overbake. Invert immediately until cool. Serves 12.

Passover Lemon Sponge Cake

This delicate lemon-flavored sponge cake makes a delightful Passover treat on its own, and is used for the Lemon Meringue Party Cake recipe to follow.

3/4	cup honey
2/3	cup potato starch
2/3	cup Passover cake meal (or 2/3 cup finely ground whole wheat matzo)
1/2	cup fresh lemon juice grated zest of 2 large lemons (yellow part of the peel)
1/3	cup fresh orange juice
1	tablespoon oil
1	teaspoon vanilla
2	egg whites
10	egg whites

In a medium-size non-stick saucepan bring the honey to a boil, and cook on low heat for 5 minutes. Use caution because honey can overflow if heat is too high. Meanwhile mix together potato starch and cake meal, and set aside. In a large mixing bowl beat the next 6 ingredients and stir in the dry ingredients just until smooth. Do not overmix.

In a large bowl of an electric mixer, beat the egg whites until foamy. While beating on the highest speed, add the hot honey in a thin steady stream. Continue beating the whites just until whites are stiff enough to hold soft peaks. Do not overbeat or cake will be too dry. Fold whites into cake batter, 1/3 at a time, just until the whites disappear.

Spread batter into an ungreased 10-inch tube pan. Gently circle through batter several times with a knife to release air bubbles. Bake cake in a 350-degree oven for approximately 45 minutes or until cake tests done. Invert cake immediately until cool. Serves 10 to 12.

Passover Brownies

Imagine what a wholesome delicious treat these brownies will be for you and your loved ones to enjoy during the holiday. Please note that this is the only recipe in our cookbook which contains cocoa. Our reason for using it in this recipe is because carob powder is not traditionally used for Passover.

2 1/4	cups boiling water
1	cup pitted dates, firmly packed
1 1/2	cups black raisins

6	egg whites
1 3/4	cups non-fat milk
1/4	cup dry non-fat milk powder
3	tablespoons oil
1/2	cup honey

1 1/3	cups Passover cocoa powder
2	cups Passover cake meal (or 2 cups finely ground whole wheat matzo)
1	tablespoon baking soda
1	teaspoon oil for pan
1	cup walnut chunks (optional)

In a medium-size saucepan bring water to a boil. Stir in dates and raisins and cook for 5 minutes. Drain, reserving liquid. In a large mixing bowl, whisk together egg whites, milk, milk powder, oil, and honey until smooth. Stir in reserved liquid. Puree cooked dates and raisins in a blender or food processor, and stir into the egg white mixture, mixing well.

Mix together cocoa powder, cake meal and baking soda, and gradually stir it into the egg white mixture. Do not overmix. Oil a 10x15-inch baking pan, spread batter evenly, and sprinkle nuts on top. Bake brownies in a 400-degree oven for 20 to 25 minutes. Do not overbake. They should be moist. When cool, cut into 2x1 1/2-inch bars. Yields 50 brownies.

Light Date Raisin Pecan Cookies

These cookies are so healthy and so delicious you'll want to make them throughout the year.

1 1/2	cups pitted dates, packed down solidly
1/2	cup black raisins
3	egg whites
2	teaspoons vanilla
1	tablespoon oil

1/2	cup Passover cake meal (or 1/2 cup finely ground whole wheat matzo)
1	teaspoon baking soda
2	teaspoons cinnamon
1/2	cup chopped pecans

6	egg whites
1	teaspoon cider vinegar
1/2	cup chopped pecans for top

(Continued)

(Light Date Raisin Pecan Cookies, Cont.)

In a blender or food processor blend the first 5 ingredients until finely grated. Place this mixture in a large mixing bowl. Mix together cake meal, baking soda, cinnamon, and pecans, and set aside. In a large bowl of an electric mixer beat egg whites with vinegar until stiff but not dry. Gently fold 1/3 of the whites into the date-raisin mixture, then gently fold in the remainder of the stiffly beaten whites. Lastly, fold in the dry ingredients, very gently, just until dry ingredients are blended.

Drop batter by heaping tablespoons on lightly greased cookie sheets and sprinkle chopped pecans on top of each cookie. Bake cookies in a 350-degree oven for 25 minutes, or until light golden brown on top. Yields approximately 30 cookies.

Individual Pear & Pecan Souffles

These delicately flavored gourmet pear souffles make the perfect ending to a festive holiday meal.

    6   large, green, firm D'Anjou pears

    1/2 cup honey
    1   tablespoon cinnamon
    1/2 teaspoon ginger
    1   tablespoon lemon juice
    3   tablespoons potato starch

    1/2 cup chopped pecans
    2   tablespoons Passover cake meal (or finely ground
            whole wheat matzo)

    5   egg whites (2/3 cup)

    1/3 cup chopped pecans for top

Cut unpeeled pears in half, core and seed them, and carefully scoop out pulp leaving skin of pear intact as a shell to hold filling. Arrange pear shells in a 10x15-inch baking pan.

Chop pear pulp in a food processor or blender, but do not puree pulp. In a large non-stick pan combine chopped pear pulp and the next 5 ingredients. Cook over medium heat, stirring occasionally just until mixture thickens. Remove from stove, and stir in pecans and cake meal.

In the large bowl of an electric mixer beat egg whites until stiff, but not dry. Gently fold whites into the pear mixture. With a large serving spoon, divide filling into pear shells. Sprinkle chopped pecans on top. Bake pear souffles in a 400-degree oven for 10 to 12 minutes or until tops are light brown. Serve warm or cold. Serves 12.

Sweet Walnut Passover Rolls

These substantial flavorful rolls can be enjoyed for lunches or with any meal.

    8   egg whites
    2   tablespoons oil
    2   tablespoons lemon juice
1/2 cup honey

    1   cup Passover cake meal (or 1 cup finely ground
         whole wheat matzo)
2/3 cup potato starch
    1   tablespoon baking soda
1/2 cup chopped walnuts

In a large mixing bowl whisk together first 4 ingredients until frothy and thoroughly mixed. Mix together the cake meal, potato starch, baking soda and nuts, and add all at once, mixing just until smooth.

On a 10x15-inch lightly oiled or non-stick baking pan drop batter into 8 large mounds. Moisten finger tips with cold water, then flatten tops and smooth sides forming rolls in the shape of English muffins. Bake rolls in a 400-degree oven for 12 to 15 minutes or until light golden brown on top and sides. Yields 8 rolls.

Quick Onion Cheese Passover Buns

These buns take minutes to make. They can be cut in half and used for sandwiches during the holiday.

    1   cup low-fat cottage cheese
    6   egg whites
    2   tablespoons oil
    2   tablespoons honey or Raisin Puree (see chapter on Basics)
         grated zest of 1 large lemon (yellow part of the peel)

    1   cup Passover cake meal
    2   teaspoons baking soda
    1   tablespoon onion powder

In a blender or food processor blend the first 5 ingredients until smooth. Pour this mixture into a large mixing bowl. Mix together cake meal, baking soda and onion powder and add, all at once, while stirring constantly until cake meal is blended. Have a 10x15-inch non-stick, or lightly oiled baking pan ready. With wet hands form the soft dough into balls. Arrange the balls spaced evenly apart in the baking pan, and press the balls down, forming flat cakes approximately 1/2 to 3/4 inch high. Bake buns in a 450-degree oven for 15 minutes or until deep golden brown. Do not attempt to remove them from the baking pan until they are cool. Yields 8 buns.

Passover Biscuits

These tender biscuits can be prepared quickly and eaten for breakfast, lunch, and for snacks.

- 8 egg whites
- 1 teaspoon cider vinegar

- 3 tablespoons honey
- 2 teaspoons lemon juice
- grated zest of 1 large lemon (yellow part of the peel)
- 1 tablespoon oil

- 1/2 cup potato starch
- 1/2 cup cake meal (or 1/2 cup finely ground whole wheat matzo)
- 2 teaspoons baking soda

In a large bowl of an electric mixer beat egg whites and vinegar until stiff, but not dry. Stop mixer, and on lowest speed, fold in next 4 ingredients. Mix together potato starch, cake meal and baking soda and gently fold in dry ingredients just until blended. Drop batter by rounded tablespoons on a non-stick or lightly oiled baking sheet. Bake in a 400-degree oven for 10 to 15 minutes or until golden brown. Yields 10 to 12.

Passover Onion Rolls

These tasty rolls can be cut in half and enjoyed for lunches with a variety of fillings.

- 8 egg whites
- 2 tablespoons oil
- 2 teaspoons cider vinegar
- 1/4 cup honey
- 1/4 cup water

- 1 cup Passover cake meal (or 1 cup finely ground whole wheat matzo)
- 2/3 cup potato starch
- 1 tablespoon baking soda
- 2 tablespoons onion powder
- sprinkle of onion powder for top

In a large mixing bowl, whisk together first 5 ingredients until frothy and thoroughly mixed. Mix together the cake meal, potato starch, baking soda and onion powder, and add, all at once, mixing just until smooth.

On a 10x15-inch lightly oiled or non-stick baking pan drop batter into 8 large mounds. Moisten finger tips with cold water, then flatten top and smooth sides forming rolls shaped like English muffins. Sprinkle each roll with onion powder. Bake rolls in a 400-degree oven for 15 to 18 minutes, or until light golden brown on top and sides. Yields 8 rolls.

Chapter 9

Basic Recipes

For your convenience, in this section we have grouped together recipes called for in more than one recipe. The Fruit-Sweetened Oat Bran Granola, for example, is called for in cookie recipes and crust recipes. Another example is the Sweet Cinnamon Pastry Dough which is used as a base for several marvelous pastry recipes.

Whole Wheat Pastry Dough

This easy-to-prepare healthy pastry dough can be used for Whole Wheat Sticky Buns and other delicious pastries.

1	cup warm water (105 degrees)
1	teaspoon honey
3	envelopes active dry yeast
6	egg whites
	grated zest of 1 orange (orange part of the peel)
3	tablespoons dry non-fat milk powder
1/3	cup honey
3	tablespoons oil
2	tablespoons cinnamon
1 1/2	cups warm non-fat milk
3	cups whole wheat flour
3	cups whole wheat pastry flour

In a small bowl mix together the warm water and honey. Stir in the yeast. Allow yeast to stand for 15 to 20 minutes until it foams up.

In a large mixing bowl, whisk together next 7 ingredients until frothy, then beat in yeast mixture. Add 3 cups of the whole wheat flour, and beat well with a whisk for 3 minutes, then add the 3 cups of pastry flour one cup at a time, stirring with a fork until flour is well blended. Cover bowl and keep dough in a warm place until double in bulk. Punch dough down. If dough is too soft to handle, chill the dough in refrigerator or freezer for 30 minutes, then roll dough out on floured board and use in various recipes. Use as little flour as possible. Yields dough for 48 pastries.

Sweet Yeast Pastry Dough

This sweet whole wheat pastry dough is perfect for Pastry Buns with Cheese Raisin Filling and other wholesome mouth-watering pastries. This dough is moist and soft, and must be chilled well before handling.

1/2	cup warm milk (105 degrees)
2	envelopes dry active yeast
1/4	cup honey
2	egg whites
3	tablespoons dry non-fat milk powder
	grated zest of 1 large lemon (yellow part of the peel)
3	tablespoons oil
2	cups whole wheat pastry flour

In a large bowl of an electric mixer, stir yeast granules into warm milk, and set aside for 5 minutes. Add honey, egg whites, milk powder, grated zest and oil and beat mixture until blended. Stir in pastry flour and beat batter for 5 minutes on medium speed. Cover and keep dough in a warm place until double in bulk. Punch down dough and chill or freeze the dough until ready to use in your favorite recipes.

Sweet Cinnamon Pastry Dough

This sweet pastry dough can be used for the Poppy Seed Pastry Ring and other wholesome pastries.

1 1/4	cups non-fat milk, scalded and cooled to 105 degrees
3	envelopes active dry yeast granules
1/2	cup honey
3	tablespoons oil
4	egg whites
	grated zest of 1 large lemon (yellow part of the peel)
2	cups whole wheat flour
1/3	cup dry non-fat milk powder
2	tablespoons cinnamon
2	cups whole wheat pastry flour

In a large mixing bowl, stir yeast granules into warm milk. Whisk in next 4 ingredients and beat well. Mix together whole wheat flour, milk powder and cinnamon, and add, all at once, beating with a whisk for 3 minutes. Stir in pastry flour with a fork, until soft dough forms. Cover, and keep dough in a warm place until double in bulk. Punch dough down. If dough is too soft to knead, then chill it for 30 minutes in refrigerator or freezer, knead the dough for 10 minutes then use in various recipes.

Whole Wheat Low-Fat Pie Crust

Most pie crusts call for at least 1/2 cup of shortening or butter. Ours has 2 tablespoons of oil, and is made with wholegrain flour. You can use this crust for any of your favorite pies. Double this recipe for a double crusted pie.

1	cup whole wheat pastry flour
1/2	teaspoon baking powder
1	tablespoon frozen concentrated orange juice
1/4	cup non-fat milk
2	tablespoons oil
1/2	teaspoon oil for pie pan

In a medium-size mixing bowl, mix together flour and baking powder. In a small bowl combine the orange juice, milk and oil. Gradually add this mixture to dry ingredients, stirring constantly with a fork until blended. Bring dough together into a ball, and roll out dough between 2 pieces of wax paper to form a thin crust to fit bottom and sides of a 10-inch deep-dish glass oven-proof pie plate. Remove top piece of wax paper, and fit crust into oiled pie plate. Carefully remove the second piece of wax paper. Turn overlapping dough under, and flute edge with finger tips. Prick crust with a fork. Bake crust according to instructions for each pie. Yields 1 crust.

Fruit-Sweetened Oat Bran Granola

This delicious tasting wholesome granola can be used on its own as a breakfast food or in a variety of recipes.

4	cups raw rolled oats
1 1/4	cups oat bran, or unprocessed millers wheat bran
2	tablespoons cinnamon
1	teaspoon coriander
2/3	cup frozen concentrated apple juice

In a large mixing bowl mix together the first 4 ingredients. Stir in apple juice until mixture is evenly moistened. Spread mixture in a 10x15-inch non-stick jelly roll pan with 1/2-inch sides. Bake in a 350-degree oven for 25 to 35 minutes turning granola over several times until golden brown. Cool and store in refrigerator. Yields 6 1/2 cups.

Soft Meringue Torte Shell

This lovely and innocent torte shell can be made ahead of time and frozen. It can then be filled with a variety of delicious fillings.

- 8   egg whites
- 1/3 cup honey
- 1   teaspoon lemon juice
- 2   teaspoons cornstarch or potato starch

In an electric mixer beat egg whites until foamy. Gradually beat in the honey and lemon juice and continue beating until egg whites are thick and glossy. Fold in starch. Gently spread mixture into a 10-inch springform pan, hollowing out center and mounding mixture around outer edges to form a shell. Bake at 250-degrees for 1 hour and turn off oven. Allow meringue shell to stay in oven for at least 1 hour or longer before removing. When cool freeze in spring form pan until ready for use.

Giant Soft Meringue Party Shell

This lovely meringue party shell can be made ahead of time and frozen. It can then be filled with a variety of delicious fillings, or garnished with fresh fruit.

- 3/4 cup honey

- 12 egg whites
- 1   teaspoon cream of tartar

In a medium-size non-stick sauce pan, bring the honey to a boil, then continue cooking it over low heat for 5 minutes. Use caution as honey can overflow if heat is too high.

In an electric mixer beat egg whites until foamy. While beating on highest speed add hot honey in a thin, steady stream. Continue beating egg whites until very thick and glossy. Gently spread mixture into a 10x15-inch lightly oiled non-stick jelly roll pan, hollowing out center slightly and mounding mixture around outer edges to form a border. Bake at 325 degrees for 20 minutes.

Reduce oven temperature to 175-degrees and continue baking the meringue for 10 minutes longer. Then turn off oven. Allow meringue shell to stay in oven for at least 1 hour or longer before removing. When cool, refrigerate or freeze in springform pan until ready for use.

Flavorful Vanilla Pudding

This delicious low-fat vanilla pudding is a perfect filling for the Giant Soft Meringue Party Shell, Strawberry Custard Trifle Pie, and Elegant Trifle.

1	cup non-fat milk
1/2	cup honey
1/2	cup dry non-fat milk powder
1 3/4	cups non-fat milk
5	tablespoons cornstarch
1/4	cup water
2	teaspoons vanilla
1/4	teaspoon nutmeg

Bring water to boil in the bottom of a double boiler. Meanwhile blend the first 3 ingredients in a blender or food processor until smooth. Pour this mixture into the top of double boiler, and stir in remaining non-fat milk. Cook over medium heat stirring occasionally for 15 minutes.

Mix together cornstarch with water until smooth. While stirring vigorously with a whisk to avoid lumps gradually stir this in, and continue cooking pudding over low heat for 10 minutes longer, stirring occasionally. Remove from heat, stir in vanilla and nutmeg, and chill. Yields 3 1/2 cups.

Date Carob Fudge Frosting

What a thrill to be able to enjoy this thick heavenly fudge frosting made without fat, cholesterol or sugar. Spread this frosting generously over Carob Cupcakes, Fruit Sweetened Date Carob Brownies, and Three Layer Date Carob Fudge Cake. As this frosting will thicken as it cools, it should be spread on the cake while still warm. If it is too thick, it can be softened with the addition of 1 or 2 tablespoons of boiling water.

2	cups pitted dates, packed down
1/4	cup water
4	tablespoons carob powder
2	tablespoons dry non-fat milk powder
1	teaspoon dark molasses
1	teaspoon vanilla
1/3	cup boiling water

In a covered saucepan, over low heat, simmer dates in 1/4 cup water for 8 minutes. In a blender or food processor, puree dates with the liquid. Beat in the remaining ingredients until frosting is smooth. Yields 2 cups frosting.

Orange Honey Sponge Cake

This flavorful sponge cake can be used to make the Elegant Trifle and Strawberry Custard Trifle Pie. Please remember that sponge cakes made with honey and whole wheat flour will not rise as high or be as light as those made with sugar and white flour.

1/2	cup cornstarch or potato starch
1 1/2	cups whole wheat pastry flour
2	teaspoons baking powder
1/4	cup frozen concentrated orange juice
1/4	cup water
1	tablespoon lemon juice
4	egg whites
1	teaspoon vanilla
	grated zest of 2 lemons (yellow part of the peel)
	grated zest of 2 oranges (orange part of the peel)
1/2	cup frozen concentrated orange juice
1/2	cup honey
10	egg whites

Mix together cornstarch or potato starch, flour and baking powder, and set aside. In a large mixing bowl, whisk together next 7 ingredients until blended. Add dry ingredients, all at once, stirring only until smooth. Do not overmix.

In a medium-size non-stick sauce pan, bring orange juice and honey to a boil and cook for 5 minutes over low heat. Use caution as the honey-juice mixture can overflow, if heat is too high.

Beat egg whites until foamy. Drizzle in the hot honey-orange juice mixture in a thin steady stream, and continue beating until whites are stiff enough to hold soft peaks. Do not overbeat whites, or cake will be too dry. Gently fold whites into the batter 1/3 at a time. Spread mixture into an ungreased 10-inch tube pan, and bake in a 350-degree oven for approximately 35 minutes until light golden brown, or until cake tests done. Do not overbake or cake will be too dry. Serves 10.

Homemade Cinnamon Apple Sauce

This applesauce is delicious on its own, and as an ingredient in several recipes. You may wish to double the recipe.

    6   small red or golden delicious apples

    1/2   cup frozen concentrated apple juice
    1   tablespoon cinnamon
    1/4   teaspoon nutmeg

Cut apples into quarters and remove core. Peel may be left on. In a 4 to 5 quart saucepan, cook apples with the remaining ingredients, over medium-low heat, for 25 to 30 minutes or until apples are soft. Cool for 15 minutes and then puree apples in a food processor. Yields 2 1/4 cups.

Raisin Puree

For those who prefer not to use honey, this sweet raisin puree can be used in place of honey in many recipes. This recipe can be doubled or tripled.

Raisin puree is less sweet than honey. Do not attempt to substitute this for honey in meringues, souffles or sponge cakes because it won't work. It can be used in many breads, muffins and cakes. Frozen concentrated fruit juices are another alternative to consider.

    1   cup black raisins, packed down solidly
    1 1/2   cups water

In a medium-size non-stick saucepan, bring raisins and water to a boil. Continue to cook over medium heat for 10 minutes, or until raisins are well plumped and some liquid still remains. Cool for 10 minutes, then puree mixture and store in refrigerator to be used as needed. This syrup keeps for 1 to 2 weeks. Yields 1 cup.

The Index